11 Things You Absolutely Need to Know About Selling Your Business

Completely Revised Second Edition

John F. Dini, CMBA, CBI

First Edition with Carlos Zubillaga

11 Things You Absolutely Need to Know About Selling Your Business

iUniverse books may be ordered through booksellers or by contacting:

iUniverse
1663 Liberty Drive
Bloomington, IN 47403
www.iuniverse.com
1-800-Authors (1-800-288-4677)

ISBN: 978-1-4502-5024-5 (pbk)
ISBN: 978-1-4502-5026-9 (cloth)
ISBN: 978-1-4502-5025-2 (ebk)

Printed in the United States of America

iUniverse rev. date: 8/10/10

Introduction to the Second Edition

In 2005 we wrote the first edition of *"11 Things You Absolutely Need to Know About Selling Your Business"* as a practical guide to the process of putting your company up for sale. It was intended simply as an educational piece to help our business brokerage clients understand the step-by-step process of selling a small company to a third party. I had a few hundred copies printed, and that was supposed to be that.

In my work with The Alternative Board® I've come to know hundreds of business coaches and peer group facilitators throughout North America. I gave copies of the book to a number of them, so that they could help their business owner clients who were preparing to transition from the business. They started calling and asking if they could purchase additional copies. Eventually we made the book available on Amazon so that we didn't have to pack and ship orders.

In the five years since it was first published, *"11 Things"* has sold thousands of copies by word of mouth and to folks who searched Amazon for a simple guide to the selling process. Although I deliberately kept the first edition short, it sacrificed a number of details in the interests of keeping it quick and readable.

I began speaking to groups of business owners and university entrepreneurial programs about selling a small business. A lecture is far more flexible than a book, and I found myself adding details and stories to illustrate the concepts. After a while the original book merely covered the high points of what I was presenting.

The world has changed a lot in the last five years. The business community is far more aware of the giant wave of Baby Boomers who are preparing to exit their companies. Third party financing for small business acquisitions has become more difficult to obtain in some sectors of the market, and more available in others. There is a new generation of buyers entering the marketplace who are very different than the entrepreneurs of the last forty or fifty years.

Most importantly, the environment of selling a business is changing. The Internet has made research about both buying and selling a key component of each sale. A buyer can quickly look at hundreds of prospective acquisitions, and compare your business to others in the same market or industry. Sellers can advertise their business for sale nationally and internationally with just a few hours' effort.

Selling a small business has become both easier and harder. It requires more preparation and better planning than it did just a few years ago. As I worked with owners seeking to transition, I also realized that the information in "11 Things" simply wasn't enough. They needed more guidance before they started the sale process if they wanted to maximize the financial results.

This second edition addresses more of the beginning of the process, and fills in some of the areas that were too brief, according to our readers. It is more than just an update. It's a complete reworking of the approach, focused on what it takes not just to sell a business, but to sell it with the best outcome you can reasonably expect.

Although this edition is lengthier than the first, I've tried to keep to the plain talk and practical language that drew so many compliments in the first book. I hope you enjoy it, and that it helps you in the most important financial transaction of your life.

John F. Dini, CMBA, CBI

1. When Should I Sell My Business?

Selling your business is the most important single financial transaction of your life. For a very few of us who were born with great wealth, are successful serial entrepreneurs, or who hit the lottery that may not be true; but for 95% of us there will only be one exit from the company you built. The years of effort have hopefully paid well as you went along, but most of us are planning a good portion of our retirement around the proceeds from selling the business.

There is an old saying that goes "When is it the best time to fire a salesman? ...It's the very first time you think about it." The idea is similar when it comes to selling your business. The first time you have a rough day and think... "*I don't want to do this any more.*", the first time that you look at your employees and wonder... "*Are they better off than I am?*", the first time you look at an opportunity to grow and think... "*Being bigger would just mean more work and more responsibility.*", it is time to start planning for the sale of your business.

Selling is much more than a transaction. It is the process of making your company presentable, desirable, marketable and financeable. It's knowing who your buyer is and how much he or she can pay. It is understanding what is valuable in your company, and what isn't. Selling your business starts with the decision to sell...someday. From that point on, you should be preparing for the transaction phase, but the transaction phase is the end game, not the whole game.

Hundreds of small business owners have asked me "What do I have to do to make my business ready to sell?" Fortunately, the answer is very straightforward. **To get the most value when you sell your company, do everything that you should be doing anyway to make your business more successful.** What is good for you is good for the buyer. It is that simple.

What do you think is worth more to a buyer: a business that depends on the owner for every decision, or one that doesn't? Would you pay more for a company that had every procedure documented, so that a new owner could look up anything he or she needed to know? Would you perceive more value in a bunch of employees who did only what they were told, or ones who could make good day-to-day decisions while you were on vacation?

Would you be more likely to buy a business that had strong financial statements or one where the owner could only verbally describe (wink…wink) all that he was taking "off the books"? Would you prefer increasing to shrinking margins? Would you rather have a diversified customer base, or one big customer that dictated terms?

The answers are so plain that it probably sounds comical just asking the questions, but many business owners don't think that way. They control every aspect of the business personally (and maintain a crushing personal workload,) by hiring the cheapest talent with which they can possibly get by. They load up the company expenses with personal items to save a few bucks in taxes. They skimp on sales and marketing unless revenues begin to slide, and then skimp on it some more because they don't have any "extra" money.

The best time to sell your business is when you don't have to. Many business owners are reluctant to sell in good times because they are making a lot of money, and won't sell in bad times because they can't get full value. **The best time to sell any business is when you <u>want</u> to. If you have made the business attractive to the right buyer; that time can be any time you choose.**

Remember; every business owner will exit his or her company sooner or later. It's up to you whether you want it to be on your terms, or on someone else's.

2. The Boomer Bust

Much has been said about the coming glut of retiring Baby Boomers. The generation that began in 1945 started reaching 65 years old in 2009. The United States Boomers represent the biggest financial event in history. By some estimates, they will transfer over *ten trillion dollars* in assets ($10,000,000,000,000) over the next twenty years.

I know that a trillion dollars isn't what it used to be. Before the latest Wall Street bailout and government economic stimuli, we seldom heard the term trillion. Now it has become commonplace in the daily news. It is still a lot of money for people like you and me, however.

The Boomers impacted everything with a pig-in-the-python effect. When they were born, their mothers bought millions of copies of Dr. Benjamin Spock's 1946 book *Baby and Child Care*, which told them that children should be raised as individuals. Dr. Spock taught that parents should be flexible regarding their children's needs. Discipline was to be used sparingly, and without anger. The Boomers were raised to believe that they were the center of the universe. In many ways, it was true.

As they grew up, the Boomers triggered explosions in school and highway construction, drove the expansion of suburbia, and made mega-industries out of toys (Mattel) and children's entertainment (Disney).

Time passed, and the Boomers enrolled in college at unbelievable rates, pushing growth in community colleges and universities. Then they entered the job market. Corporations which were previously bastions of the nine-to-five workday and the gold watch at retirement were inundated with ambitious and educated young men, and for the first time young professional women, who all expected to climb to the corner office with a big expense account.

There wasn't room for <u>everybody</u> in the big corporations, but the Boomers had come to expect that they could have it all. So they opened businesses in record numbers. Many did not have the basic business skills to be entrepreneurs. To serve this growing market, franchising was born and quickly became the dominant business model in many retail and service markets. For the first time, you didn't have to know everything about a business to own one. Small business ownership could be taught.

The Boomers became consumers. Suburbia pushed out to Exurbia. Savvy marketers catered to Boomer wealth with ranchettes and McMansions. Boomers worship youth and vitality, so the self health market once limited to One-a-Day vitamins mushroomed into exotic supplements, health clubs and personal trainers. Retail space *per person* in the US increased by over 250% between 1986 and 2008.

Now the Boomers are preparing to retire. They own more businesses than any generation before them, or probably than any in the future. The Baby Boomer business owners face a challenge like none other. Just as they have done everything else together, the **Baby Boomer business owners are all going to sell their companies at the same time.**

Whether you took Economics in high school or not, you've heard of the Law of Supply and Demand. It says the more that is available to sell (supply) the lower the price becomes. It also says that the fewer buyers there are (demand) the lower the price becomes.

What happens when the supply (Baby Boomer Sellers) goes up a lot and at the same time demand (Generation X Buyers) drops off rapidly? It isn't going to be a pretty picture for sellers of small businesses, but you can still beat the odds.

It is easy to understand why the Boomer owners selling in lock step would raise supply, but why would the demand fall precipitously at the same time? Let me introduce you to Generation X.

Generation X, or GenX as the marketing folks would say, is the group immediately following the Boomers. Logically, they would be the next generation of business owners. That isn't going to happen for most of them, and there are a number of reasons why.

GenX was raised by the Boomers. Focused on their own success, the Boomers married later and had fewer children. So a generation of 78 million people is being followed by one of only 46 million. Demand is naturally lower when you have 40% fewer buyers.

Fewer available bodies means that there will be growing competition for employees. As the Boomers retire from the corporate world, they will have to be replaced. Large organizations can offer far greater benefits and compensation than a small business could possible offer and, in many cases, more than even the typical small business owner receives. Those who search for business buyers will be competing with those searching for business executives.

The most important issue, however, is the preferences of the GenXers themselves. GenXers have not been raised as entrepreneurs. They don't find the same gratification in owning a business, are less inclined to take risks, and have different priorities than the Boomers.

Most Boomer business owners have complained about their younger employees from time to time. Some say that GenXers don't have the same work ethic, or they don't have the same ambition. What the Boomers don't understand is that GenX was raised differently from the Boomers, and has a different set of core values.

GenXers are more comfortable in their skin than Boomers. Raised by Boomer parents who made sure that they each got a trophy just for being on the team, GenXers expect to be appreciated for anything they do. They were taught to expect love for who they were, not for what they did. They were told that work wasn't life; it was merely the means that funded the rest of their lifestyle. For the "I am what I do" Boomers, it often doesn't make a lot of sense.

Logical or not, GenX doesn't have the numbers, the need, or the inclination to do anything that takes too much effort, pays too little, or stresses them out. They look at the hours, the compensation and the pressure of being a small business owner, and they simply don't get it. There are so many easier ways to make a living.

Add those three factors together and you will have a buyer base that shrinks dramatically over the next 20 years, just as the supply of businesses for sale explodes.

Until now, Boomers have been buying businesses for a second career, and selling their businesses to other Boomers. Once the boomers finally stop buying, the world of small business sales will change dramatically. Like any market under pressure, quality rises to the top. **If you want to be a successful seller, you'll need a business that GenX will want to buy.**

That will have to be a business that provides a good living without killing the owner. To rephrase what I said in Chapter One, the best way to prepare your business for sale is to make it into the kind of business that you wouldn't want to sell.

3. The First Thing You Need to Know: Understand the Process of a Business Sale

Valuing Your Business

Business valuation is not an exact science, but arriving at a reasonable price is the first step in selling any business. Different valuation approaches estimate the market value of a business from different points of view. The most common methods, discounted cash flow analysis, multiples of earnings, multiples of cash flow and comparisons with prior sales of similar businesses (comparatives or "comps") are widely used and easily calculated.

Most small companies are sold as a multiple of the amount of benefit the owner is taking from the business. This is commonly termed Seller's Discretionary Cash Flow (SDCF), Seller's Discretionary Earnings (SDE) or sometimes just "free cash flow." All three terms mean the same thing, and we will stick with SDCF for this book. **SDCF is the amount of money that the owner takes out of the business including salaries, bonuses, taxes and any other benefits received by the owner and his or her family plus interest, depreciation, amortization, and the net profit shown on the Profit and Loss Statement.** Using a multiple of SDCF has long been the most common practice in small business valuation.

There are other terms frequently used in business valuations. EBITDA is Earnings before Interest, Taxes, Depreciation, and Amortization. This is a measure of a business' ability to generate cash from operations, but doesn't encompass salary or any additional benefits being taken by the owner. EBIT is a stricter measure which assumes that depreciation and amortization are normal costs of doing business, and thus ignores them in profitability.

These earnings measurements are more commonly used for larger companies where ownership is clearly divided from management. SDCF is appropriate in businesses where the owner is the principal manager, and the buyer is assumed to be an individual who expects to make his or her living by operating the business personally.

The most frequent argument of small business buyers (and their attorneys and accountants) is that the SDCF earnings need to be adjusted for the cost of a manager. The counter argument is that businesses that have separate ownership and management sell for higher multiples of EBITDA than the multiples used for SDCF-based transactions.

The two approaches aren't interchangeable. One is appropriate for one kind of business, and one for the other. In this book we are discussing the sale of your business, which you presumably own and operate personally. In a few areas where there might be a difference for larger, professionally managed companies, I will point it out.

Setting Your Price

Once you have arrived at a realistic estimate of market value for your business, you can make a more informed decision about your asking price. Business owners frequently confuse the value of the business with their desire to walk away with a specific amount in their pockets. They ultimately ask a price based more on their feelings than on any objective estimate of what the business is worth to a prospective buyer.

It is customary to advertise the asking price of smaller businesses. As the size of the business reaches "middle market" (businesses selling for over $3,000,000), the common practice is to ask for bids from interested buyers, rather than advertising the asking price, and let the market set the price, preferably by competition between multiple buyers.

For sales where the target buyer is an individual who will run the business as his or her livelihood, the asking price should pass a

"Buyer's Sanity Check." The sanity check is a means to determine whether the asking price will make economic sense to the purchaser. The SDCF of the business should cover debt service from any loan used in the purchase, provide a reasonable return on investment for the buyer's invested capital, and leave sufficient excess to provide the new owner with a decent living. I will further discuss the details of pricing strategy in Chapter 5.

Defining Your Strategy to Sell

Setting your price is only the beginning. In order to navigate a successful sale process, you'll need to figure out the following:

- Recognizing and qualifying your prospective buyers (Chapter 6)

- Preparing effective marketing and sales materials for your business (Chapter 7)

- Understanding the underlying tax issues that drive negotiations (Chapter 8)

- Comprehending the parameters and hot buttons of third party lenders (Chapter 9)

- Collateral and security for seller financing (Chapter 10)

- Deciding whether to use a business broker (Chapter 11)

- Structuring the mechanics of a deal (Chapter 12)

- Due Diligence (Chapter 12)

- Managing professional advisors and other stakeholders in the sale (Chapter 13)

Preparing the Information Package

Even the best defined strategy for selling your business will still require terrific supporting materials. Your company presentation package for prospective buyers exemplifies the old adage *"You never get a second chance to make a first impression."*

Dealing with prospective buyers requires several different presentation packages for marketing, presentation, and due diligence:

> a) One package with general information (which may or may not identify your business) available to the interested parties.

> b) A Confidential Business Review, or memorandum, describing the business in detail.

> b) A complete package of confidential information for qualified buyers who have signed a non-disclosure agreement. This package includes your financial statements, tax returns, and enough proprietary information to allow the prospective buyer to analyze the business in depth, make an offer, and prepare for due diligence.

> c) Due diligence materials which may include both redacted and complete versions of proprietary data, and may be released at different milestones in the process (See Chapters 7 and 12).

Advertising the Business for Sale

Most business owners want the sale kept confidential until a deal is certain. Premature word of a business for sale can disrupt relationships with customers, vendors, competitors, and employees. Unlike a home, businesses don't place "For Sale" signs on the front lawn.

On the other hand, unless the business is advertised as being for sale, potential buyers will be limited to those who can be reached directly or through word of mouth. Internet web sites are the most common and effective way of advertising businesses for sale. Specialized trade publications can be selectively used, as well as general-purpose media. Each company may require a different advertising strategy, depending on whom you have identified as a prospective buyer (See Chapter 6).

Advertising budgets for several principal web sites and newspaper ads can range from a few hundred dollars to $20,000 or more.

Advertising a business is usually done without naming the specific company for sale. While this approach can generate a lot of interest, it also brings inquiries from casual shoppers and curiosity seekers. As the owner, it is in your best interest to treat every inquiry as serious until you have qualified the "suspect" as a prospect.

Dealing with Interested Prospects

Dealing with prospects is challenging and time consuming. **Avoid wasting your time with unqualified buyers by developing a planned approach to qualification.** General information, without identifying the business, can be made public via advertising to attract interest. Interested parties are supplied with an initial package of information, usually after signing a non-disclosure agreement.

Qualifying a buyer is a critical part of the process. If you have a methodology for testing and confirming qualifications, you'll save many wasted hours in unproductive meetings.

If a prospect expresses interest in pursuing a purchase after receiving your initial information, he or she must be qualified as financially able to complete the purchase. In most cases a buyer seeks to finance a substantial portion of the purchase price through seller and/or third party financing. The "bankability" of the prospect is the single most important factor in screening and qualifying buyers (See Chapters 6 and 8).

For most business owners, dealing with aggressive prospects is a harrowing process. Many buyers begin their negotiations with unrealistically low opening offers, or by criticizing the business in an attempt to position their first offer. You must be able to separate your emotional attachment to the company from the bargaining.

Objectivity is often the greatest value that a professional intermediary brings to the negotiating process.

Negotiating an Offer

An initial offer is usually made via letter of intent. This should outline the purchase price, terms of payment, estimated closing time, and any contingencies. Many sellers stop marketing their business once they receive an offer. Remember, *a majority of initial offers do not result in a sale.* While you are negotiating, you should continue to actively market the business and deal with other prospects.

Negotiating an initial letter of intent is less than half the battle. Buyer and seller must then create a definitive agreement, with contingencies for financing, due diligence and deadlines. Finding a willing buyer is frequently the easiest part of the sale process. The execution of a successful transition still lies ahead (See Chapter 12).

Once the essential terms of the deal are agreed between buyer and seller, contracts must be drafted by an attorney with experience in the transfer of privately held businesses.

For smaller transactions, I recommend that both parties agree on a neutral attorney to draft the documentation and act as escrow agent, if such is permitted by state law. Appointing different attorneys for the two parties and going back and forth between them in negotiating the documentation, as is customary in larger transactions, can run the legal bills up to amounts disproportionate to the size of your deal. I've seen transactions of less than $200,000 run up legal costs of nearly $30,000. Know how to utilize your attorneys appropriately in the transaction (See Chapter 13).

Obtaining Financing for the Buyer

Failure to obtain financing by the buyer is the single most common deal killer. Sellers can waste many hours dealing with unqualified buyers. The most important attributes of a qualified buyer are the ability to make a down payment to the satisfaction of the lenders, and prior experience in a similar business.

Down payment requirements will vary greatly depending on the characteristics of the deal, but 20% to 50% of the purchase price is typical for a (healthy) small business.

Many lenders prefer to see at least a portion (10% or more) of the sale price held as a note by the seller. Friends and associates may advise you to "always get all cash," but that simply isn't realistic in many small business transactions (See Chapters 9 and 10). In fact, a buyer who has all cash typically expects a substantial discount from the asking price.

As the seller, you probably feel that financing is the buyer's problem. That is technically true, but in reality you have a vested interest in helping with the process. While the buyer is seeking financing, your business is usually off the market, since most Letters of Intent require a "stand still" agreement. This is a condition that the seller ceases negotiations with any other buyers while the deal is being finalized. If the buyer fails to qualify, you are starting the marketing and sale process all over again. **You are the most important factor in obtaining financing for a qualified buyer.**

Due Diligence

Simultaneous with the search for financing the purchase, the buyer performs due diligence on all the elements of the transaction. This usually includes detailed inspection of your financial information, tax returns, personnel administration, title to assets and facilities, sales records, physical inventory, and analysis of accounts receivable and accounts payable.

The purpose of due diligence on the part of the buyer is to validate the information you've provided to a point where the buyer feels reasonably comfortable and understands the risks involved in the purchase. In virtually every transaction, the buyer's offer is contingent on the results of the due diligence process.

Many sellers resent a buyer's repeated requests for more information. Remember that many things which may appear obvious to you may not be so clear to an outsider. The buyer's lender can also generate a large number of requests for documentation. Preparing and providing due diligence materials can be a major distraction to running the business. The more documentation you have prepared prior to listing the company for sale, the easier your due diligence process will be.

I will discuss preparing and presenting your documentation for due diligence at length in Chapters 7 and 12.

Closing the Sale

Once a deal has been struck between buyer and seller, financing for the buyer becomes the most critical factor in successfully closing. The demands of a lender, combined with discoveries during due diligence, frequently create additional elements to be negotiated, and lengthen the closing process. The quality, thoroughness, and reliability of the information provided by the seller to the buyer, together with a properly screened and qualified buyer, make the whole process more predictable and bearable.

A large number of acceptable offers disintegrate during the due diligence phase. Buyers grow suspicious about delayed or incomplete data. Sellers become irritated by "unreasonable" requests for details and supporting documentation. Emotions run high between one party who is giving up his livelihood, and the other who is risking his.

Closing a transaction can be a circus. The stakeholders and other impacted players (see Chapters 11 and 12) include brokers, attorneys, vendors, customers, employees, insurance companies, accountants, landlords, regulators, bankers, and a host of others. Someone has to quarterback all the efforts of the team.

If you are utilizing the services of a professional business intermediary, he or she may help you with much of the due diligence documentation process. If you are not hiring a business broker, consider using your attorney or certified public accountant (CPA) as an intermediary. Many sales collapse "at the altar" because one party says something impulsive or ill-advised to the other in a moment of stress.

The remainder of this book will walk you step-by-step through the process of selling your business. It isn't easy, but it is within the abilities of anyone who has hired, fired, trained, motivated, bought, sold, targeted prospects, closed deals, and collected money.

In other words, if you own a small business, you can sell a small business. You may not want to do it by yourself, but you clearly need to be in charge and control the process. You are entering into what is probably the most important financial event of your business career. In order to do it successfully, you first have to understand the process.

4. The Second Thing You Need to Know: What Will You Do Tomorrow?

Selling your business can be a painful process. You are emotionally attached to your business and you may be uncertain about what to do after you get it sold. **If you haven't planned for the next phase of your life, separating from your business will be a much more challenging process.**

You must be prepared to detach yourself from the emotions of giving up the "baby." Making some decisions in advance regarding what you will be doing after the sale is completed will make for a more relaxed and smoother sale process.

Many brokers will refuse to take a listing from sellers who have no clear idea of what they will be doing next. Such sellers are much more likely to find excuses to delay a sale, make unreasonable demands, or simply bolt from the process as the closing approaches.

A few years ago, my company was asked to represent an owner who had been approached about selling. Although asking about life after the sale is a key component of our initial discovery, the person handling the transaction was anxious to land the deal, and ignored that step in our process.

We thought the company would probably sell for between $6,000,000 and $6,500,000. The broker handling the sale for our company did a great job of marketing, and wound up with two publicly traded companies bidding for the business. We were all pretty excited when two firm, written offers came in on the same day. The first was for $11,700,000 and the second a few hours later was for $11,400,000. We were definitely on track for a home run!

Then the owner disappeared.

He didn't exactly disappear. We knew that he was at his business every day. He just made himself invisible to the broker. He was too busy to take the calls, and stopped responding to emails.

After a week or so the broker drove down to the business to stake it out until the owner finally spoke to him.

"I can't do it," he said. "I wake up every morning with the same thought in my head. If I didn't go to work today, where would I go? Tell them the business is off the market."

He is still working there today. He doesn't work hard, and he doesn't need the money. He just needs somewhere to go.

People who haven't owned a business frequently compare it to building your own home. That barely scratches the surface of what a business means to its founder.

In your business, every aspect of the company reflects your ideas, your vision, and your talents. You picked the business, most likely because of skills or experience that you had. You hired the employees, trained them, and communicated how you wanted things done and why.

You picked the location, negotiating the lease or purchase of the property. You probably bought or approved the purchase of every piece of equipment and stick of furniture in the building.

You chose the market and the target customers. You made the company's first sale, and probably many more after that. You pitched the customers on why they should do business with your company, and then made certain that they didn't regret their decision.

You sourced the products and chose the service vendors. You wrote the policies, procedures, and job descriptions.

You've probably counted a number of your closest friends among customers and vendors who you've known for years. In that circle of friends and acquaintances you are universally known as "Bob Smith, the owner of Smith and Company."

Your business is part of you as nothing else is part of you. It's a reflection of your ability. It is your life's work. It is your public identity. Without your company, who are you? It's a question you'll need to answer if you are going to be happy at the closing table.

How many business owners have you known who were unhappy in their "retirement"? Entrepreneurs aren't generally idlers by nature. They are motivated, and need to be busy. As more than one retiree has told me six months after selling, "You can only play so much golf."

As a business owner, you have spent most of your business life looking forward. Entrepreneurs function much better when they are moving *towards* the future, rather than *away* from the past. Understand what your future holds, and you will experience far less pain in separating from your company.

Talk to your spouse and your friends. What do they think you'll do after the sale? Sometimes the people you know best see talents or skills that you have taken for granted or overlooked in the course of running your company every day.

If you haven't yet discovered your passion outside of the business, now is the time to think about it. Give it a trial run to see if you really like it. More than one owner has thought that he or she would like woodworking, or traveling the country by RV, or teaching a class, only to find out too late that it wasn't really what he or she expected.

I have known dozens of business owners who wound up working for their old companies, simply because they didn't know what else to do to stay busy.

Make sure to consult your financial advisor. Will the proceeds from selling your company provide you with the means for a different lifestyle? Many sellers are disappointed to learn that the net after-tax cash from a sale will leave them needing additional income. Sometimes, they discover this too late to stop the sale of the business without risking litigation.

When planning your financial future, be realistic about the proceeds of a sale. A few years ago I spoke to a group of financial planners. Over two thirds of the group (there were about 30 planners there) agreed that they were planning for business owner clients who had more than half of their net worth in their companies. To my surprise, *not one* of those planners had ever sought a third-party opinion of that value. They were relying entirely on the owner's belief about what he could realize from a sale.

Half of their clients' retirement plans, half of their future lifestyles, half of their legacy to their children, was based on a number that may or may not have had the slightest resemblance to reality. That's why the third thing you absolutely need to know is how much your company is actually worth.

5. The Third Thing You Need to Know: Value and Pricing

What is my business worth?

The first thing most prospective sellers ask me is "How much is my business worth?" There are a number of ways to arrive at an appropriate number, but let's talk first about the ways you <u>shouldn't</u> use.

Hearsay is the bane of any broker's existence. "I heard that a guy in my industry sold his company for four times revenues." "Everyone in my business gets at least six times profits." "A publicly traded competitor is valued at 23 times earnings on the market. I must be worth at least *half* of that."

First, forget the multiples that at which publicly traded companies sell. The liquidity of the markets, equity leverage and pricing in predicted forward earnings projections have nothing to do with small business. **Your business is valued by how much the new owner thinks he can make from operating it.**

Then forget 90% of what you heard about other sales. I had a professional tell me recently that he had sold his business for one and a half times his gross revenues. That is the rule of thumb in his industry, and is frequently cited for many other professional practices like CPAs and insurance agencies.

Because he is a friend, he let me look over the deal after it was done. Yes, the price was 150% of gross revenue. There was very little money down; just enough to pay the legal and accounting bills. The rest was based on installments over the next three years.

The balance of the note on which the installments were based was adjustable monthly, depending on client retention. The norm in his industry is 25% annual turnover, so he could expect to collect the full amount on about a quarter of his clients for the full three years.

He was also required to continue working part time for those three years at a greatly reduced income. He didn't mind. After all, he was really partnered with the buyer in keeping the clients happy, since their continued satisfaction would determine his final price for the business. He was just a financial partner without much control or say in running the business that used to be his.

Was that a bad deal? No. After three more years of work, he will probably walk away with almost as much money as he would have made if he had continued operating the business full time, he will cut back his work load substantially, he avoided suddenly having nothing to do, and he <u>will</u> get to walk away. The deal fulfilled his objectives.

Was he lying about the valuation? No. He *sold* the business for 150% of gross revenue. What he will *collect* is probably more like half of that, and he will have to work a few more years to realize even that much.

This illustrates a fundamental truth about hearsay valuations and rules of thumb. **Sellers will always claim to have received the highest price for their businesses that they can possibly justify.** Everyone wants to look successful, especially someone who is putting a value on his life's work.

Sale Price Assumptions

Most small businesses are valued and priced net of current assets (other than inventory) and debt-free.

Current assets include cash in the bank, marketable securities owned by the company (not common in small business), and accounts receivable. These are the results of business conducted prior to the sale, and are rightfully the property of the seller. If you maintain substantial cash for working capital, or carry large receivables balances, keeping these items will be part of your compensation in a sale.

Inventory is usually included in a sale, but you'll need to specify the level of goods on hand that the buyer should expect to be included in the purchase price. Inventory above or below that level will require adjustments to the price at close.

The buyer usually seeks to assume the assets debt-free. You will be expected to use the proceeds of the sale to pay off any liens or notes on assets. As always, everything can be (and usually is) negotiated, but assumption of debt is commonly considered as part of a purchase price.

In a stock sale (See Chapter 8), the current assets and all liabilities transfer with the ownership. If you are involved in a stock sale, both parties will negotiate carefully around the balances of cash, inventory, debt, and accounts receivable to be available at the time of close.

Fair Market Value

The most critical step in selling a business is to know how much it is worth. The relevant number here is the fair market value. ***Fair Market Value*** is defined as:

> ***"The price a willing seller and a willing buyer, both possessing complete information, agree on; when there is no undue pressure to act on either side."***

Regardless of the valuation method, the market eventually determines the price to pay for any given business regardless of the value of its assets or other pricing equation. Often business owners are disappointed when they learn that the value the market assigns to the business differs greatly from the value that he or she expected. Whatever you feel is the "right" value for your business, the final price will be influenced greatly by the economy, availability of financing, and the number of similar businesses for sale in the same market.

The first step to any successful sale is some sort of valuation of your business. Valuations can be formal or informal. Informal valuations, usually performed by accountants or business brokers, are most commonly used to sell a privately held business. Certified appraisers perform more formal valuations, usually with some type of legal purpose such as in estate, litigation or divorce related situations.

The value of any business depends on its ability to generate income after the sale. In some cases, the assets of the business are critical to it, but don't represent the best use of capital.

I had a seller with a construction business that required substantial earth moving machinery. He loved his big toys, and was constantly buying and selling both new and used equipment.

He also hated, absolutely hated, the idea of employees standing around doing nothing. So he had developed a "system" where he would move an excavator and a bulldozer to a job site a few days before it was needed. This way he could transport the employees to the site and have them working from the minute they arrived.

The equipment on the completed job site would frequently stay there for a few days (or weeks) after the work was done. He had plenty of equipment to go around, and he was usually in no hurry to pick it up.

With a double set of machinery, along with the additional spares and whatever was in the process of being sold, he had over $1,500,000 worth of heavy equipment. Unfortunately the business was only generating around $150,000 a year in cash flow. He couldn't comprehend why his business wasn't even worth the value of its working assets.

Regardless of any targeted multiple of earnings, every business has to pass the Buyer's Sanity Check. That means that the price paid must be low enough to provide three things to any buyer:

- Sufficient cash flow to cover debt service

- An appropriate living wage for the owner of the business

- A return on the capital invested sufficient to justify the risk

When you look at the value of the business, consider the return on investment for your assets. Many owners, once they have paid off the debt on their assets, lose the discipline of making them produce to their capacity. "It's here, it's paid, and therefore it's free," may be a rationalization for you to accept a lower return, but the logic evaporates when a buyer is calculating <u>his</u> return on what he pays you for those assets.

Buyers perceive the risk of owning a business to be high. Risk, or "beta" in the stock market's terminology for the volatility of an investment, has a range. The lowest risk is usually considered to be in U.S. government bonds, which are safe and stable. The debt of foreign countries, states and municipalities has a slightly higher beta. Investing in a publicly traded stock is higher yet. Putting money into a small business, which lacks the liquidity, financial underpinnings or guarantees of any of the previously mentioned investments, is usually expected to return between 25% and 50% annually "cash on cash" for the funds invested.

The valuation of any business is influenced by the purpose of the valuation, the methodology used, and the objectives of the person who will be using the valuation. Sometimes your business has to be right-sized to get a valuation that makes sense. In the case of the dirt contractor, I recommended that he sell a substantial amount of the equipment, pocket the money, and offer the business at a price more in line with its earning ability.

Valuation Methods

Three criteria can be used to estimate the fair market value of a business: income, assets, and market comparisons. Each has a different purpose, and using the wrong approach in a sale can be costly.

Valuations for legal purposes have a very different purpose than those for a business sale. Valuation professionals who are certified by their professional association include the designations CVA, AVA, ASA, and ABV (See glossary). These professionals are required to use specific methodologies that will be accepted in a court of law, and must be prepared to defend their opinions on a witness stand.

Unless you are getting a valuation for a divorce, an estate dispute, or an unfriendly partner breakup, such "certified" valuations are probably not necessary. They can be expensive (typically 5 figures and up) and may not be the most accurate way to price your business.

Many business brokers also do business valuations, although those certified by the International Business Broker Association (IBBA) are forbidden by the code of ethics from tying the cost of a valuation to a sale listing. In other words, if a broker says "I'll charge you $3,000 for a valuation, but if you give me the listing it is free," he would be violating the IBBA's Code of Ethics. That doesn't mean that he is a crook, but it at least means he doesn't know his industry's professional rules.

It is common, however, for a broker to charge market rates for a valuation, and credit it against his commission on a sale. This isn't an ethical violation, since the payment for the valuation is separate from the listing and sale process. If he fails to sell your business, the appraisal was paid for, and would stand on its own.

The Income Method of Valuation

The income method (the most common in privately held business transactions) generally uses a discounted cash flow methodology, which puts a value on the income stream that the business will produce in the future.

In the income method, the valuator assumes certain levels of profitability for a specific period of time, generally from seven to fifteen years in the future. The total of those profits is then discounted by an imputed interest rate. The imputed rate represents the amount that it would take to earn that amount of cash in another investment.

Typically, the imputed rate represents a risk-free return (Treasury Bills) plus a premium for risk. And that, ladies and gentlemen, is where the fun begins. How much is an appropriate risk premium for owning a small business? When you compound over time, a few points difference in the imputed rate yields a huge difference in value.

A low rate renders a very high value. To make it simple, any amount of money at zero interest is worth just as much today as it will be in 15 years. So a zero interest/risk rate results in valuing money that you will get 15 years from now as worth exactly the same as if you got it today. Intuitively you can understand why money in your hands today is more desirable than waiting fifteen years for the same amount.

A high interest/risk rate, therefore, gives little value today to cash that's expected years down the road. If you had a cost (or risk of losing it all) of 20% every year for the next 15 years, you would probably pay nothing for the opportunity.

I have to take a side trip here for a moment to warn you about something that happens to sellers every day. There are several organizations in the US that offer seminars on how to value your business. First the attendees are asked to calculate their cash flow into the future, assuming that the company continues to grow at a healthy rate. They then use the discounted cash flow methodology, imputing an interest rate that is very low; comparable to bank lending rates. They point out that strategic buyers will pay seven to eight times cash flow for businesses. (That is sometimes true, but more about strategic buyers later.)

The owners walk out with stars in their eyes, certain that they have just been given the inside secret to why their businesses are worth millions of dollars more than they thought. That's when they get pitched on the $30,000 engagement to prepare their company for sale.

Of course once that engagement is paid for, the consultant often discovers that *your* company has special issues and problems that just won't support those kinds of price assumptions. So sorry.

There are three fallacies in the approach. First, no buyer is going to pay you for increased sales after he owns your company. He thinks (legitimately) that since he is then running the business, those profits should be his.

Second, the risk premium for a small business is much, much more than a bank's lending rate. The higher the imputed interest, the less a dollar in the future is worth today. Most valuation experts will use no less than 15%, and many use rates as high as 25%. High-risk investors, like venture capital firms, use rates of 33% and more.

Third, discounted cash flow and multiple of earnings are two different valuation methods. You can't add up the value of future earnings and then multiply them. They are two different approaches to reach the same thing - an approximation of value. You don't add the two methods together.

Finally, be very skeptical of people who tell you that higher valuations can be expected from mysterious overseas buyers. The biggest advisory firm in Europe is Price Waterhouse - an American firm. Tokyo, Bangkok, and Shanghai all have offices of the same investment bankers and financial advisors found in New York, Chicago and Atlanta.

Wealthy foreign businessmen have the same advisors and expect the same return on their investments as Americans. Few wealthy people, whether Americans or not, got that way by being fools.

The Asset Method of Valuation

A business can also be valued by looking at the fair market value of the assets, minus the liabilities. Fair market value in a business sale means the cost of replacing those assets with what is termed "like-used" assets, or similar equipment of similar age bought on the open market.

In an asset valuation all values are net of liabilities. This means that you have to subtract any outstanding debt that you used to finance the purchase of an asset from the market value. In the case of rapidly depreciating assets, like a delivery truck with high mileage, the value can be lower than the money owed on it.

Don't confuse market value with depreciation. Depreciated value is a tax device to estimate the impact of an asset's use on profitability. Tax accounting has little to do with actual asset values.

For example, I had a construction client who used a military surplus tanker truck in his business. Built to Army specifications for hostile environments, this little 1961 beauty had a solid stainless steel tank and ten wheel drive. The engine had been rebuilt four or five times, but the rest of the vehicle was essentially indestructible. It had been depreciated down to zero a dozen years before, but its "like-used" value was still significant.

Business brokers who do valuations will frequently take the owner's estimate of what assets are currently worth. If you are seeking a more accurate and defensible estimate of the current market pricing for capital equipment, I recommend using a Certified Machinery and Equipment Appraiser (CMEA). These are usually business brokers who have been separately certified in researching the prices for used equipment.

Asset methodologies usually understate the true value of a business. In a service business, which includes most of the businesses in this country, there are few assets on which to put a value. In many other businesses well maintained equipment can be expected to perform for much longer than its projected lifespan.

A typical mistake that many sellers make is to value the cash flow of their business, and then add the assets to get a price. The assets are what generate the cash flow, not a separate transaction. There are valid reasons to use either the asset method or the income method to value a business but again, you can't realistically add them together.

The Market Method of Valuation

Finally, the market method of valuation looks at how similar businesses have been valued by the market in the recent past and applies comparative ratios or multiples to the business being analyzed.

There are a number of ways to determine comparatives. Some are very accurate, and some less so. The most accurate are the proprietary databases of private business sales, such as Pratt's Stats and BizComps. These are maintained by companies that service the business brokerage and merger and acquisition (M&A) industries.

Although these databases are self-reporting and self-policing, it is in the interests of the contributing professionals to provide accurate information. Since the data is anonymous, there is no benefit or bragging rights to be gained by inflating the numbers.

Another very accurate source of data is the business tax return databases. These, too, are subscription-based and depend on their subscribers for their data. ProfitCents, for example, collects tax return and financial statement information (without the name of the business) from thousands of CPAs around the nation.

While these databases don't have information on selling prices, you can extrapolate some values by comparing the financial results of your company with those of others of the same size in the same industry.

One good feature of ProfitCents is that it lists total owner compensation, which can be difficult to determine in a small business. Of course, you would also have to factor in any inaccuracies (perish the thought) in your tax returns!

Similar information is collected by the banks through a company called Risk Management Associates (RMA). The RMA numbers come from loan applications. They are also separated by industry, and have more revenue groupings than ProfitCents. Neither RMA nor ProfitCents has selling prices, however, and RMA only reports the owner's income from the salary line of the tax return.

Probably the least accurate measure of comparison is the information collected (and widely publicized) by the business-for-sale websites. The information that they make available for free is typically the asking price for businesses by region and industry. Since there is no restriction on who can list a business for sale, or how much they can ask, these numbers are seldom anywhere near reality.

Whatever the method used, it is important to point out that it is the market value and not the seller's subjective value that counts. A business owner's emotional involvement in the company often reduces his or her objectivity when considering its true value in the marketplace. Regardless of how much you thought you would get, were told you could get, or feel you need in return for your life's work; the Fair Market Value of your business is exactly what someone will pay for it.

Seller's Discretionary Cash Flow

A discounted cash flow method is most commonly used for small business valuations. It attempts to define the economic generating capability of the business as a multiple of the earnings generated for the owner. It is based on the income method, but with special inclusions that recognize the realities of small business ownership.

Small businesses do many things at the owners' discretion when it comes to expenses. Your company may provide unusual benefits or employ family members. You may combine a business trip with personal travel, or drive a company vehicle that's a bit more luxurious than is strictly necessary.

These can be valid and legal benefits of owning your own business. Your company provides a quality of life to you, the owner. That is part of your business' value. **All of the financial benefits that accrue to the owner should be calculated as part of the economic generating capability of your company.** Before selling your business, it's necessary to "recast" your financial statement to show the true cash flow of the company. As I mentioned earlier, there are a number of similar terms for this number, but we will stick with Seller's Discretionary Cash Flow (SDCF).

The SDCF concept shows a buyer what funds will be available to pay for new debt, personal salary, and as a return on his down payment investment. It takes your decisions about spending the cash generated by your business, and couches them in a format in which he or she can allocate them as (s)he sees fit.

SDCF is the single most important factor in selling a small business. SDCF starts with the company's profit as shown on the tax returns, and adds back owner's salary, benefits, bonuses, distributions, and any other financial benefits paid for by the company. It also includes income taxes, interest expense, and non-cash expenses such as depreciation or amortization.

You may be asking "How can I show interest expense as income? That seems like it's artificially inflating my profits." There is logic to the add-backs that may not be apparent at first glance.

Interest expense is added back because financing business expenses is an ownership decision. You need a piece of equipment to expand. You could pay cash, but that may require money that would otherwise pay your salary. You could defer the decision, but that would mean missing an opportunity. So you decide to borrow the money for the purchase, with the reasoning that the new equipment will return more profit to you than the interest absorbs.

Since your business will most likely be transferred without debt, the decision to invest some of your income to finance faster growth or bigger profits shouldn't result in a penalty when it comes to valuation.

Depreciation and amortization are tax accounting devices. As we said earlier, tax accounting should have little to do with how you actually run the business. Since they are non-cash deductions from income, they are typically added back in to show the cash available for debt service.

Adding back an owner's discretionary expenses requires judgment. There are some add-backs, like a nice company car, that are widely seen as perquisites of the owner and considered acceptable when looking at the cash flow available. (That's assuming, of course, that the new owner doesn't expect to be driving that car after the sale.) When you take recast statements to a bank, you should be aware of what they will find acceptable and what will set off alarm bells.

Surprisingly, family members who receive salaries for vague jobs that have little or no function in the business can often be recast as earnings. Many financiers will accept an explanation (delivered with a smile) that employees having the same last name as the current owner will not be employed immediately following the transaction.

On the other hand, I know a businessman in Texas who writes off almost $10,000 annually on his personal "work boots." He really does purchase the boots, but they tend to come in exotic leathers like ostrich and boa constrictor, and he seldom wears them to work. Showing these as income would raise a red flag for a banker, since it might indicate that there were other questionable items in the company's financial statements.

Don't get too wrapped up in finding items to recast. A calculation of SDCF that includes dozens of minor expenses will give a buyer the impression that you are trying to squeeze profits into your calculations to inflate the price. Stick to fairly legitimate, major expenses.

When you begin preparing to sell, review all the extras you are taking from the business, and eliminate those that may be in a gray area. Since a typical small business will sell at between two and three times its SDCF, you are better off showing those items on the profit line than making weak explanations as to why they should be considered.

Buyers and banks are rightfully wary of companies that show their profitability based only on internal statements. Use your tax returns as the starting point for all SDCF and debt service cash flow calculations. Buyers and banks place greater trust in your tax returns, because they know that there are legal penalties for falsification of your IRS submissions.

Factors Influencing Price

In small business transactions (valuations roughly under $3,000,000), the business has a price tag and it is usually advertised for sale at the given price. In larger transactions, also called "middle market" deals, the business is usually offered for sale without an asking price. Information is given to the buyers who then make bids on the basis of their own analysis.

The three major factors driving the value of a privately held business are the SDCF, the management team, and the management systems. While cash flow is king, the other two factors can help to increase the value of your company for a prospective purchaser.

Individual buyers will first look at the disposable cash flow that the business generates. They will assign more weight to recent periods, particularly the last two to three years. The quality of your financial information is a key element that lends credibility to your cash flow figures.

A buyer will also look closely at who in the company (besides the owner) possesses the know-how that makes the business function; and the caliber of those key people. The more dependent the business is on the owner, the harder it will be to sell.

Key employees are assets, and their quality impacts the selling price of your company. Their length of employment, specialized training, age, and commitment are factors in their value. Written employment agreements for critical performers and strong incentive compensation increase a buyer's comfort level.

Many sellers keep the sale of the company secret from the employees for as long as possible. While I understand an owner's concern with creating uncertainty in the workforce, that isn't always the best idea. Consider sitting down with your employees and explaining how the sale of a company is a normal part of the business life cycle. It allows them to keep their jobs as the business continues after you no longer wish to run it. Give them time to get used to the idea.

If the employees are aware of the sale, it is much easier to introduce them to potential buyers, and potential buyers *always* want to meet the key employees at some point in their due diligence process. Also, if certain employees are critical to your operation, you should consider signing them now to an employment agreement with a nice bonus (funded by you at the closing) to be paid if they stay for several years following the sale.

Finally, potential buyers will look at the administrative systems, financial information systems, information technology, operations, marketing, sales, and management systems and how effectively they work. They will look particularly at how people-dependent, as opposed to process-dependent, these systems are.

Buyers will assign a higher value to businesses that are run by written processes rather than by individuals with the methods in their heads. Every buyer fears that knowledge critical to the success of the business will walk out the door when the current owner leaves. The more documentation of critical knowledge and systems you can show, the higher the price you can demand.

Of course, external factors can influence pricing as well. The financial crisis of 2008-2009 made acquisition financing for small businesses very difficult, and often impossible to obtain. Buyers saw their savings shrink dramatically in the market slide, and many walked away from deals.

Another factor affecting price is the need for licensing or certification to operate the business. If you are the only qualified license holder in the business, your company will be much more difficult to sell.

Dependence on a single customer, volatile prices for key commodities, or a very narrow niche in a market dominated by a much larger player will all detract from the desirability of your company.

On the positive side, many things that at first glance look negative may help you in selling the business. A recession, for example, may mean layoffs of many corporate executives who are unable to find replacement jobs. They often look for a small business to buy, both for income replacement, and because they have developed a strong aversion to being at the mercy of someone else's cost-cutting decisions.

The Dismal Ds

Unfortunately, many businesses are put up for sale because of the "Dismal Ds." These are factors that depress value in a company, and include Declining sales, Dissention among owners, Disinterest, Disaster, Distraction, Debt, Divorce, Disease, Disability, and Death.

If you are selling your company because of the Dismal Ds, take an objective look at your business. **If sales, operations, margins, or profits show a declining trend, expect a buyer to discount an offer to compensate for his increased risk.**

Many sellers want to disregard the Dismal Ds when selling the company. They feel that their business performed well for years, until the event that created the decline. Buyers, however, know that a company with excellent employees, management, and systems might not have seen the impact on profits that the Dismal Ds can cause.

Many of the Dismal Ds are events over which you have little or no control. Disinterest, however, is one that you can anticipate. When an owner tells me that she is "burned out" I know what I'll usually find when I look at the financial statements. The burn out began years before, and the results show it. Remember what I said in Chapter 1; it is far better to sell your business before you've driven yourself past your last ounce of enthusiasm.

It seems unfair that an unfortunate event can create the "double whammy" of both reducing the current returns from your company and discounting the equity that you've built up over years. Buyers aren't interested in fairness, however. They are interested in buying a successful business.

Many buyers ask a price for their business based on what it used to be. They argue that it had a long track record of success, and that new ownership could quickly restore its former success. That may be true, but the buyer isn't going to pay you for his restoration effort. The business you are selling is the one you have today, not the one you had a few years ago.

If you are considering a sale because of the Dismal Ds, price your company realistically. Having your business linger on the market while its value declines further merely makes the inevitable outcome worse.

The biggest factor in any transaction is the seller's ability to wait for the right buyer. If you are under time constraints to get out of the business, whether from outside forces or your own needs, expect to discount the price in direct proportion to the speed you are seeking.

Disappearing Cash

There is no law against having two sets of books. There is a law against fraudulent bookkeeping. The deductions you make for tax purposes may or may not be discretionary. You may choose to attend one trade show a year in Hawaii, or have your daughter on your Board of Directors, which meets at Disneyland. Those are tax-deductible expenses, as long as they are within the guidelines of the law.

What you cannot do is take cash out of the business without recording it. No legitimate broker or accountant will attempt to help you to justify a sale price for your business based on unrecorded cash.

Since businesses usually sell for two, three, or four times the SDCF, decide which is worth more to you; a dollar in your pocket today, or four dollars in the sale price? If you are planning to sell your business, start recording all the revenue. Owners who sacrifice profit multiples in a sale for a few dollars out of the cash draw are only stealing from themselves.

Cash can be a great aid to real profits when it is unaccounted for, but it also creates a lot of questions in a buyer's mind. Employees or vendors who are paid under the table, customers who receive secret cash discounts and improvements made for less than the market cost all leave a buyer wondering if he will be able to run the business profitably without all these special arrangements.

6. The Fourth Thing You Need to Know: Buyers

There are five kinds of business buyers; internal buyers, entrepreneurs, professional investors, industry buyers, and strategic buyers. **The objectives, motivations, and ways of doing business are different for each type of buyer.** Decide in advance who your most likely buyer will be. It can save you time and money in marketing your business for sale.

Internal Buyers

For many companies, an internal buyer is the most logical option. **A key employee, or group of employees, often has the operating knowledge and customer contacts to keep the business running successfully.**

A sale to internal buyers brings a unique advantage. It is the method in which the seller usually has almost complete control of the process. You set the price, the terms, and the date you want to leave.

The first option that I explore with a business owner who is thinking of selling is the viability of an employee purchase. There are usually three objections; lack of talent, lack of desire and lack of money. While all are valid concerns, they can often be addressed.

The first is a lack of talent. "Bob's a great worker," I hear "but he doesn't have the decision making ability to run the business."

Ask yourself this: How good were you at making decisions the day you started your company? Did you know it all on the day you walked in, or have you learned through experience? Did you make mistakes? Did they put you out of business? (It's obvious that they didn't, or you wouldn't be reading this book.)

So is Bob really *incapable* of making decisions, or is he just *accustomed* to having you make them for him? Would he make company-threatening mistakes, or do you just make sure that he isn't allowed to get in that deep? Don't you have him check with you on major questions? Could he be taught to make better decisions? Would he be more careful, more analytical in his decision making if more were at stake for him?

Often, the development of a key employee into a good decision maker is more a problem for the owner than it is for the employee. You have to be willing to step back, and to let Bob learn from a few mistakes. No child really understands why you say "Hot! Hot!" about the pot on the stove until he touches the pot...once. That's usually all it takes. Do your key employees really understand the long-term impact on profitability of their decisions?

If a key employee or employees can be taught your thought process in decision making, he or they may be candidates for eventual ownership.

The second objection to an internal buyer (or buyers) is a lack of desire. There may be some truth to that, but there is also some owner-ego involved. Many entrepreneurs believe that the people who work for them are *meant* to work for somebody. "If they were like me," you think, "they would open a company of their own."

It's true that many employees enjoy the security of a regular paycheck. For some it's a behavioral trait, but for many others it is economic necessity. A family, mortgage payments, and kids in college leave many folks feeling that they can't risk their regular income.

You have the same issues and responsibilities, of course. The difference between you and them is twofold. First, you believe that you can manage the risk so that your lifestyle isn't threatened. Second, you are willing to take some risks today in return for a better income a bit down the road.

If your prospective successor is worried about security, you may be able to help him or her get past that obstacle. A gradual takeover, with you there to guide and mentor, can alleviate many of their concerns about the risk.

The third reason, no money, is the one most often quoted. "Bob lives from paycheck to paycheck." "Mary just bought a new home." "Fred has a deadbeat son whose family he supports."

Internal sales usually take place over time. Employees are permitted to purchase stock for a note, and make the payments out of their share of the profits.

The owner's objection to this is obvious. "But then they are paying me with my own money!"

That is true, but it's true in every sale, regardless of who the buyer is. If you sell to a third party, they will pay the bank with the cash flow of the company. If you take a note for any portion of the sale (see Chapter 10), you will clearly be paid with your own future profits.

Owners often object to the concept of having employees as partners during the transition period, or to the risk of having to take back the company if a note payment is missed. Both are valid concerns, but what if you could control the company completely right up until the day you walked away with the full purchase price in cash?

There are methods for selling non-voting shares to employees until they have built a track record and equity sufficient to qualify for outside financing on the balance of the purchase. Consulting with a qualified business exit planner can give you a wider range of options than you may have thought possible.

The purpose behind selling your business is to exit when you wish while enjoying the benefit of future earnings. Any transaction accomplishes that in one way or another. If you have a business that is licensed or otherwise dependent on key employees, they may be your best buyer option.

You should be aware that very, very few business brokers have the expertise to assist in an internal sale. A broker is paid to market and sell your business to a third party. An internal sale takes years, and requires considerable planning. There are Certified Exit Planning professionals (CExPs) who specialize in internal transfers. Don't expect a business broker to encourage you to sell to insiders.

Entrepreneurs

Entrepreneurs are usually looking for small businesses that they will be running personally after the acquisition. In many cases, the entrepreneurial buyer is looking to "buy a job." He or she may be a downsized executive who cannot make the same salary in another job. He is planning to commit a substantial portion of his savings, and is nervous about the risk of self-employment.

In some cases, the entrepreneurial buyer owned another business prior to this. She feels that she has the capabilities to run your company, and probably has a few ideas about what she will do with it the day she takes over. Expect the experienced entrepreneurial buyer to be aggressive in identifying the faults of your company.

Be careful of wasting your time with someone who just *looks* like an entrepreneurial buyer, but really isn't. I've become very wary of the prospective buyer who tells me "For over 35 years I've had a burning desire to be my own boss." A desire that continues for 35 years is anything <u>but</u> burning. That buyer has always found a reason why it wasn't the right time or the right circumstances to own a business. He is likely to find another reason to avoid ownership before you get to the closing table.

I recently had a risk-averse buyer look at a small construction services company. He used the "I have always had a burning desire," line but was otherwise exceptionally qualified. The company had years of steady growth and increasing profitability. It had repeat customers, and licensed employees who ran the company day to day. We provided five years of financial information. The buyer asked for seven years, then for ten. He demanded an outside appraisal of the property, and then argued that the certified appraiser wasn't using the correct methodologies.

He eventually made an offer for the business. It included a condition that the seller work for him for as long as he deemed necessary, and agreed to return at any time in the future if the business ran into trouble. Obviously, the seller wanted to sell the business, not continue operating it without sharing the profits. He quite sensibly refused the offer, but a lot of time was wasted in the process.

All entrepreneurial buyers seek to leverage their purchase, so obtaining financing is an important factor in closing the sale. Generally the entrepreneur will search for the business personally, rather than retain a professional representative to conduct the search for them. The purchasing process will also be emotional, since the entrepreneur is frequently risking his or her life savings to buy your company.

Nonetheless, if your company is being sold for less than $1,000,000 the entrepreneurial buyer is your primary target.

Professional Investors

Professional investors, such as venture capitalists or private equity groups, will be looking to buy an interest (with a significant degree of voting control) in a business with good management in place. The professional investor adds value, primarily through infusion of capital and perhaps secondarily through specific industry knowledge, contacts, marketing channels, and management know-how.

Professional investors will seldom approach a business owner directly, often working through brokers or intermediaries. Some brokers will target specific professional investors, depending on the type of business that they are representing.

Professional investors are attracted to industries that they know well, and usually have a well developed formula for valuing and pricing an investment opportunity. They are particularly concerned with the company's potential for rapid growth.

It may seem illogical that such investors often prefer revenue growth over profits, but there is a reason for their approach. In a private company, profit can be manipulated by deferring expenses. Increasing revenue, however, indicates a business with bright prospects regardless of the bottom line.

Because professional investors are specifically seeking a business with strong management characteristics, they are seldom an option if you are looking to exit your business in the very near future.

Industry Buyers

Industry buyers are your local competitors or similar businesses to yours in a different geographical market. Industry buyers are looking to grow their business by acquiring other similar companies in their market, or to quickly establish a base of business in a different geographical area.

Industry buyers are attracted by a solid customer base and the potential economies of scale realized from expanded operations. They will often pay a premium for strong customer relationships, but will discount the value of your employees and systems.

The price paid by industry buyers is not as dependent on cash flow. They will create additional profitability through the economies of scale of combining your company with theirs.

Strategic Buyers

Strategic buyers are generally very large private or publicly traded corporations that have a strategic reason for buying a particular business. They are seeking to acquire a specific technology or process owned by the business being sold, acquire a presence or customer base in a geographical market, or acquire the skills of the personnel working for a particular company.

Specific features of a business that add instant value through acquisition attract strategic buyers. The value of your company may be greatly enhanced by its attractiveness to a strategic buyer. They are seeking acquisitions specifically because "the whole is greater than the sum of the parts." When dealing with a strategic buyer, you must have solid information about his or her reasons for interest, other possible deals in the offing, and pricing for previous acquisitions.

Strategic buyers are frequently experienced at acquisition. As the name implies, they have a strategy for their business that includes acquisitions, and dedicate substantial talent and resources to the effort. Because the value of the purchased business has little to do with its cash flow, they keep information about their reasoning and plans pretty close to the vest. Maximizing your sale price to strategic buyers requires research and a clear understanding of their business model. Most small business owners are well advised to hire an investment banking professional to help in the negotiations.

Strategic buyers will pay higher, and sometimes much higher multiples than any other type of buyer. Where an entrepreneurial buyer will usually pay between two and three times SDCF, and an industry buyer might pay twice that, a strategic buyer will sometimes pay eight, nine or fifteen times the EBITDA. (Notice that the method of measuring cash flow changes from SDCF to tax return based calculations when you play with the big boys, however.)

For that reason, many sellers immediately ask an intermediary to find a strategic buyer for their business, simply because they want a higher price than they could otherwise get. Making a strategic sale isn't merely a matter of finding someone who is willing to pay. You need to have a company that is sufficiently differentiated to demand a premium over others.

Gaining the interest of a strategic buyer requires both a strategic purpose and strategic value. Unless you can clearly define your strategic value to such a buyer, and back it up with excellent reasoning as to why your company fits the bill better than any other, you are wasting time chasing strategic multiples.

Ask yourself several questions before deciding to pursue strategic buyers. Do I really have a product or service that no one else can deliver? Do I have defensible intellectual property? Are my customers completely dependent on me as a sole source? Are there few or limited substitutions available for what I do? Would the target buyer be able to vastly expand my offerings to other markets or other customers? The answer should be yes to *all* of these questions to justify a strategic acquisition.

In reality, few small businesses have the resources to truly differentiate themselves. High customer service ratings or being named the best in the business by your local newspaper doesn't necessarily qualify you for a strategic sale.

Fantasy Buyers

There is a sixth buyer that I didn't list among the five types. That is the fantasy buyer. The one that all sellers hope for, but which doesn't really exist.

Every market and every industry has urban legends about buyers who have lots of money and little or no business sense. Many sellers waste time and energy seeking these fantasy buyers. In the worst cases, the buyer rejects good offers from qualified buyers in the hope that one of these fantasy buyers lies just around the next corner.

Fantasy buyers come in three flavors; hobbyists, foreign nationals, and giant corporations seeking new ideas.

Hobbyists are typified by the proverbial "Doctor's Wife" buyer. This scenario, usually found in small retail businesses, goes something like this. The wife of a wealthy physician (or attorney, or business executive) is bored with her empty country-club lifestyle, and wants something to do. Money is no object as long as she thinks that the business will be fun, and it is something that interests her. If she wishes, her wealthy husband will write a check subsidizing the purchase and any subsequent losses just to keep her happy.

The foreign national fantasy says that a wealthy rich man or woman from South America (or Japan, or Hong Kong, or Saudi Arabia) wants to buy a business to establish residency in the United

States. He or she is so rich that a few hundred thousand or a few million dollars in cost, or any minor variable such as profitability, is simply beneath his notice.

The "corporation in search of a fresh idea" fantasy says that a big player wants to buy your concept, so as to make it into a run away national success. This theory assumes that corporations don't have anyone who can actually think on their staff, and that they would never stoop to duplicating a concept once they saw it.

I remember a marginally successful restaurateur who wanted to list his business for three times its market value. He was rock solid in his belief that some giant chain would pay for his concept of an old-west themed steakhouse. The existence of four similar restaurants within a ten mile radius seemed to have escaped him.

Fantasy buyers have one trait in common. They are assumed to have a reason for buying your business *other* than owning a successful business. How many of your present customers do business with you for reasons *other* than their need for your product or service? That should give you an idea of how many fantasy business buyers are really out there.

Targeting Your Buyer

Your ability to target a specific type of purchaser is a function of the kind of business you own and the type of value you may offer to each target group. In most small business transactions, your universe of buyers will be limited to the entrepreneurs who seek to operate the business personally.

Once you understand the most likely buyer for your company, you can make decisions about how to approach the market.

Entrepreneurial buyers are best reached through Internet sites catering to individuals and through local marketing. Unless you are prepared to deal with each inquiry personally, you probably want to consider the services of a business broker or other intermediary.

There is a more complete discussion of what to look for in an intermediary in Chapter 11.

Industry buyers are most likely to be found through trade publications and professional associations. If your customer base is local, you probably know the prospective industry buyers. They are your competitors. **Many business owners are reluctant to discuss a sale with competitors, because they fear the information will be used against them in the marketplace.**

While competitive concerns are valid, don't ignore an opportunity to get a higher price because of fear. You know your competitors, and can probably identify the ones with whom you might like to work. You know the areas in which you are better than them and (shhhh!) in which they might be better than you. Which one might be a fit where the whole is greater than the sum of the parts?

Make sure to consider the age of the owner before you approach. There is no point in trying to sell to someone who may want to sell to you. If you do approach a competitor, open the discussion by asking if he might be interested in a merger. If the response is positive; begin to trade information (always using a confidentiality agreement) on a step-by-step basis. Only after you reach a level of comfort should you introduce the idea of your exit.

With this merger approach, your competitor can't say anything about you that you can't also say about him. You were just talking.

Professional investors usually represent themselves, and will make an approach or inquiry personally. **Professional Investors are in the business of buying businesses. They are far better at buying businesses than you are at selling them.** Beef up your side of the negotiating table with an investment banker, M&A specialist, or an attorney with a strong track record in deals. Too many small business owners gloat about the professional fees that they saved by doing the negotiations themselves, but leave many times that amount on the closing table.

Strategic buyers may represent themselves or use a professional intermediary. The same advice holds about getting professional help on your side from the beginning of the process.

Advertising the Sale

Spending your marketing budget unwisely can be disastrous. Spending money on worthless advertising is bad enough. When selling your company, however, spending in the wrong place can swamp you with unqualified leads, while the prospects whom you seek are finding their opportunities elsewhere.

It's surprising how many business owners are great at describing their product to customers, but list their business for sale as if the reader had magic glasses to see through to its hidden qualities.

Check your materials to see if you are discussing features or benefits. The old marketing adage, WIIFM (What's In It for Me?) applies here. Describing your company as a market leader is a feature. Explaining that your widespread reputation drives unsolicited business in the door at very low cost is a benefit.

Web Based Listings

Today, most individual business buyers start their search on the Internet. Internet listing sites are generally available to individual sellers. A few, such as the International Business Brokers Association (**www.IBBA.org**) are open only to listings by professional intermediaries.

Many trade and professional publications now maintain listings for businesses available in that industry. Such listings are usually both in the magazine and on their web pages. If you have a business that is most likely to be sold to a similar business or to someone with direct industry experience, these are often the best places to start.

Start your search as if you were a buyer. Put your criteria into an Internet search engine. What hits does it return? Do different keywords, such as your industry or location, change the results? Do one or two sites come up consistently when you use different methods?

Do sites come up because they are purchasers of key words? Watch for search combinations that return a majority of results for business brokerage networks, franchises or franchise consolidators (franchise networks that sell other franchises.) These terms (and the sites to which they lead) are of little help in promoting your business.

Once you have assembled a number of potential listing sites, look at them critically. Are they where you would want your company represented? Your business will be judged by the company you keep. Some sites seem to draw loonies. As you look through the listings, are there many that seek investors for start-up opportunities? Is there a substantial percentage of home-based businesses, or multi-level marketing deals?

Once you have narrowed the field, start looking at listings that would compete with yours for prospects. How are other businesses in your industry described? What seem to be the hot buttons? How can you differentiate your listing from all the others?

Also check businesses <u>unlike</u> yours that are geographically close and priced in the same range. They are your competition for buyers. A majority of successful buyers acquire a business other than the one that they originally examined.

If you are using a business broker, ask what sites he will include as part of his business services. You should be just as critical of his choices as you would be of your own. Just because a web site is included in the broker's fee structure doesn't necessarily mean it's someplace you want to be.

Never make a listing decision based solely on cost. The Internet, like anything else, usually delivers what you pay for. Free sites, such as Craig's List, will generate a lot of traffic but fewer real buyers.

The number and quality of leads that you will get from a top-ranked site such as www.bizbuysell.com or www.bizquest.com (two of the industry leaders) more than make up for any savings realized by listing cheaply on something like "BubbazBizsalez4u."

Print Advertising

Advertising for buyers in the local paper or business journals may be beyond the budget of an individual seller, and has limited benefit. Some brokers maintain print ads for their collective listings. These can be beneficial because a good broker will consider all prospects to be candidates for any business that he has listed.

If you choose to advertise your business individually, keep the ad to a minimum size and description. The sale of a business takes many steps, and you are only seeking to generate a phone call, not to convince a buyer to purchase a business through your advertising.

Video Presentations

A number of businesses now utilize video in presenting the company. Some brokers promote this technique as well. Unfortunately, amateurish video can greatly hurt your chances of selling for a top price.

Any prospective buyer in this century was raised in a media society. He or she is extremely aware, even if subconsciously, of the subtleties of lighting, background, furniture balance (the set), and motion on the screen.

An honest and competent business owner can look furtive or stumbling on videotape. Normally lit offices appear dark or dingy. Busy production areas may look cramped and dangerous. Grinning employees can raise suspicions about coercion or collusion.

In the long run, no video presentation will sell a company if the financial and business fundamentals are weak.

Unless you have at least $25,000 to spend on a professionally produced video, I strongly advise leaving this marketing avenue to the infomercials on the shopping networks.

7. The Fifth Thing You Need to Know: Presentation is (Almost) Everything

Many years ago, I worked for a national restaurant chain. They taught me a trick that I still use today. Walk out of your business. Stand on the street and close your eyes for 15 seconds. While they are closed, say to yourself "I need to buy a business, and I've never seen this business before. I wonder what it looks like?" Then turn around and walk back into your business with a buyer's eyes.

You never get a second chance to make a first impression. It's an old saw, but it has lasted because it is so true. **Every single step of the listing and negotiating process is being judged by the buyer for its professionalism.** Since your prospective buyer doesn't know you, he is judging the value of your business by what he sees.

Curb Appeal

Over the last decade, it has become popular to hire a stager when you are selling your home. The stager gives advice on making the house more appealing. It can range from reducing clutter on the walls to completely changing out the furniture.

Your business needs to be staged as well. Start with the exercise I described at the beginning of this chapter. What do you see? Is the front of your business clean and presentable? Is the landscaping healthy and trimmed? Are there weeds in the parking lot?

What does your entry area say about your company? Is the reception area clean and bright? A new coat of paint never hurts. Are there stacked files, blocked walkways, boxes in corners? Are there light bulbs in every fixture?

Is your inventory dusty? ("*It's probably not worth what he has it on the books for.*") Are the restrooms less than sparkling? ("*She doesn't spend any money on maintenance.*") Are your offices a monument to the durability of faux-wood paneling? ("*They haven't touched this place in years.*")

I don't need to get into a lengthy description of what an organized and efficient workplace should look like. Go though your business room by room, closet by closet, and make it as presentable as possible.

Occasionally, a business owner will tell me "I can't do anything about that. It's the landlord's responsibility." Let me ask you a question. *How much of your proceeds from the sale are you giving to your landlord?* That's what I thought. Fix it yourself if you have to, because you are the one who will reap the benefits.

Financial Records

The quality of historical financial information is the one single factor with the highest impact on the business sale process. **Solid, professional-looking financial information results in more trusting buyers, easier communications, and quicker financing.**

Inaccurate, inconsistent, or unreliable financial information creates wary buyers. They examine details more closely. Their initial offers drop, and the price that they will pay is lower because their perceived risk is higher. Third party financing becomes more difficult and more expensive. Simply put, poor quality in your financial records makes any deal more difficult to close.

Have <u>at least</u> three years of financial information copied and ready for a buyer's examination. Tax returns and financial statements should be current. Annual statements should be ready no later than 90 days after year-end, and monthly data within 15 days after monthly close. Late data indicates sloppiness in the bookkeeping process, which worries both buyers and their bankers.

The simpler you can make your information to understand, the more likely a buyer will be willing to meet your price. Graphs, charts, and illustrations help to make your financial information clearer. It is your job to make the buying opportunity plain.

Don't hide the negatives! You own a business. No reasonable buyer should expect any business to have a perfect record of untrammeled success. If you do anything, go overboard in revealing all the warts and blemishes of the business.

A good buyer will accept an explanation of why something looks less than terrific, but no buyer is happy to find out negatives for himself. It causes him to look further and deeper, in case more issues are hidden somewhere. If you are put in a situation of explaining a problem that the buyer discovered for himself, you've probably lost that buyer.

It is customary to show three years of financial data, but if there was a bad year before that, include five or six years of data in your package. You can then better explain how your business was strong enough to recover from the setback.

If your revenues are dependent on a few customers, say so up front. It will save you a lot of explanation later.

If an employee is key to the operation, say so. If your margins have narrowed, tell the prospect why before he asks.

If you've recently lost a contract, a key employee, or a product line, then say so. Don't press forward with an unrealistic presentation of the company's situation in the hope that the buyer will become so enamored that he will overlook it. When it is eventually discovered you will simply look foolish, trust will be shaken, and more time will be wasted.

A good business broker will help you to develop attractive supporting materials for your financial records. He or she should also maintain copies of your records, update them as necessary, and present them to qualified prospects.

If you are not using a broker, consider asking your accountant for help in preparing your financial documentation. The fees will be more than returned in your time and energy dealing with buyers.

Projections

Many sellers and business brokers will prepare projections describing the future prospects of the business. While this may help a buyer to conceptualize the possibilities, it can also lead you into trouble after the sale.

Always discuss the ideas that you have for growing the business. After all, if a buyer is paying for your company with the next few years' profits, he will need to understand how he can earn some for himself, too.

You probably have any number of things that you never had the time to implement, or you just didn't have the inclination to do. Make a list, with the explanation that not every one may be a great idea, but they can help the buyer to see greater potential.

Buyers will inevitably see the obvious opportunities first, and it's likely to be something that you've already tried. Don't shoot down the buyer's ideas. Be honest, but remain open to the possibility that a different owner under different circumstances might have better results.

Avoid the "hockey stick" graph. That is where you project modest increases for a few years, and then because of economies of scale or critical mass the results suddenly skyrocket. In addition, don't label future projections by year, such as 2013, 2014, 2015 etc. Either approach to projecting could result in a claim of misrepresentation if it doesn't come true.

If you are going to present projection to a buyer; label them with percentages or growth or profit. Saying "This is what would happen to your economies of scale if revenues increased by 15%," is a theoretical exercise. Presenting them as potential sales in future years could be taken as a representation if they don't come true.

Of course, the best projections are those that were documented in the past and came true. Having a written business plan with past iterations on hand is the best of all possible projections.

Supporting Documentation

Before you begin the sale process, it is wise to assemble all the documentation that a buyer will need to close the transaction. **Make copies of everything a buyer might need for due diligence.** Quick response to document requests builds buyer confidence, and speeds financial approval.

Some of the items you'll need to prepare include:

- lists of assets used in the business
- employee payroll information
- equipment and property leases
- distribution or franchise agreements
- supplier and vendor contracts
- accounts receivable and payable detail
- customer lists
- sales history and product movement data
- inventory turnover and ageing
- shareholder agreements and corporate filings

Remember, not all of your business information is appropriate to share at once. Some items are shared as part of the initial presentation process (such as asset lists), some are shared during due diligence (leases, contracts, and agreements), and some, such as proprietary systems and customer lists, often aren't shared until the closing.

The closer you get to a completed sale, the more information you'll need to share. If one thing is guaranteed, it's that a buyer will want to see more than you want to show him, and see it earlier in the process than you think is appropriate. Selling your business involves an extended period of negotiations, and much of it revolves around your supporting documentation.

Some documentation can be delivered in pieces. For example, most buyers will want to know a lot about your employees. It is usually appropriate to deliver a list showing the number of employees, their positions, and their pay rates right after receiving a letter of intent. It isn't necessary at that time to reveal the names of each employee.

After the buyer has a financing commitment in hand from a lender (if necessary), it is usually time to sit down and discuss the employees individually. If the buyer wants to meet and discuss employment with key people before the close, it is important to document what will or won't happen as a result of those conversations. It is not unheard of for a buyer to say that retaining an employee isn't important, only to call off the deal when that employee resigns as soon as he or she is notified.

The same step-by-step approach to key information can be used with customer lists, pricing and proprietary processes.

Presentation as Marketing

Many sellers go to lengths to present attractive financial statements, and then provide supporting documentation as a hodge-podge of original documents, duplicates, and electronic files. Gather your documents in a single format. If documents are scanned or in electronic files, many professional business brokers will provide a password-protected online repository for them.

Most business owners understand the value of attractive marketing materials in selling their product or service. Surprisingly, they fail to apply the same standards to their biggest sale of all - that of their entire company.

You may consider your financial records boring and mundane, but they are far from it to an interested buyer. Your leases and contracts may have been gathering dust in a file cabinet for years, but they are new and important factors in your buyer's decision making process.

Look with a fresh eye at how you present your information. Are you copying copies of copies? Is your photocopier producing documents with streaks or shadings? Is your printer old, and obviously of a lesser quality than what is currently used in most businesses?

Copying and printing equipment that serves you well for day-to-day operations may not be the quality needed for presentations to a buyer. If that is the case, consider retyping documents before you present them. Even legal contracts are better presented in a readable version with a copy of the signed original attached. If you don't have the capability to make quality copies in-house, spend the extra few dollars to have it done at the local photocopy shop.

As I indicated above, a good scanner, or having original documents scanned, can save a lot of time and trouble. It is a one-time cost for unlimited use. It also creates an impression of competence and efficiency when a buyer asks for information and you provide it a few moments after the phone call.

Try to make every step of the discovery process a pleasant surprise to the buyer. It may not make the price go up, but it can stop him from looking for reasons to make it go down.

8. The Sixth Thing You Need to Know: Taxation Drivers

The complex issues of taxation become even more confusing when a business transfers ownership. **Both buyers and sellers need expert tax advice in relation to several key considerations impacting a sale.**

Many business owners wait until they have a contract for sale before they tell their accountants. This has always mystified me, since once you have a contract it is usually too late for good tax advice. Spending a few hundred or a few thousand dollars up front can reap great rewards.

Stock vs. Asset Sales

The Federal Tax Code and IRS regulations are designed to create opposing interests between buyer and seller in relation to the basic structure of a sale. Because the size of the transaction is substantial, the taxes are due immediately, and both parties document the funds involved carefully, the IRS sees business sales as an area that can be clearly and efficiently monitored.

The structure of a business sale is pretty much a zero-sum game from a tax standpoint. Classifying purchase price items as capital gains (a lower tax rate) for the seller usually results in lower write-offs for the buyer. Using methods that allow rapid expensing against profits for the buyer typically puts the seller's income into a higher tax qualification. **Deciding whether your business should be sold as a stock or an asset transaction will usually be determined by factors other than tax impact.**

The seller typically prefers a stock sale. The seller's gains on a stock sale are generally taxed at a more advantageous long-term capital gain tax rate. A stock sale is often easier, since the seller doesn't have to deal with canceling contracts, terminating employment, or reconciling vendor accounts.

A stock sale may be dictated by the need for continuity in insurance or bonding, maintaining long-term contracts, to preserve special status with Federal and state governments, or to keep a license active. Absent these conditions, however, an asset sale is usually a cleaner and safer way to transfer a business.

On the other hand, the buyer is encouraged by tax regulation to favor an asset purchase. An asset purchase allows the buyer to book the assets at the purchase value, an advantage in calculating future tax-deductible depreciation.

In addition, a corporate entity transferred by stock purchase continues to carry all the liabilities from the previous ownership. A buyer often prefers to get a "fresh start" with vendors and customers after a change in ownership. Forming a new entity allows him to establish new relationships with key business suppliers.

Most small, privately held businesses change hands to third parties as asset sales, while stock sales predominate in family or employee sales.

Despite the preponderance of asset sales in small business, many CPAs and attorneys seem to derive a twisted enjoyment from torturing sellers with what might have been. I can't count the number of calls I've gotten from sellers saying "My attorney says I should have gotten a stock deal. He says I'm giving the IRS 20% more for <u>nothing</u>."

Usually, the seller has conveniently forgotten our conversation as to why an asset sale was necessary. He's also assured me that he talked it over with his CPA before we listed his company. In fact, I've *been* in those pre-sale conversations with a seller's CPA, and *still* gotten the call. In the negotiating process sellers frequently focus on price and terms, forgetting the tax bite that is inevitable.

Unlike the income tax you paid while running your business, the proceeds from a sale can't be reduced by a little expense here and a financing technique there. The IRS pays attention, and has made sure that almost anything that reduces taxes for one party raises them for the other.

Your business should be priced with full knowledge of what the tax implications will be. I've seen sellers walk away from great deals because they had an erroneous understanding of how much they'd get at the end.

Think through why each part of the deal was agreed to before you present an asset sale agreement to your CPA or attorney, only to hear "This is a terrible deal! You could have saved a lot of money by making this a stock transaction!" Asset deals are asset deals and stock deals are stock deals for very good reasons, and tax consequences are only one of them. Make sure you understand how your deal is structured and <u>why</u>.

Corporate Structures

Your corporate structure can greatly affect the tax treatment of the transfer. A "C" corporation (a "regular" corporation) is taxed at the marginal income tax rate on gains over the depreciated book value of the assets. As the owner of the corporation, your distributions of the proceeds are taxed again as ordinary income. This double taxation leaves many sellers greatly disappointed when they discover the percentage of their sale proceeds destined for government coffers.

Other structures, including Sub-chapter "S" corporations, partnerships, and Limited Liability Companies can generally avoid double taxation. Multiple structures, such as a captive equipment leasing company, may offer substantial tax reduction options.

"C" corporations can be converted to a different type of entity, but there are complications. The value of the business at the time of conversion is subject to the Built-In Gains (BIG) tax if there is a sale. The BIG tax is gradually reduced over the ten years following the conversion.

Some tax advisors will advise you not to make the change from a "C" corporation if a sale is anticipated in just a few years. That never made much sense to me, since the tax is calculated on the value at time of conversion. If your company's value increases at all over the next few years, there is no BIG tax on those gains.

By the time you list your company for sale, it is usually far too late to change your corporate structure. Careful planning a few years in advance, however, can save you substantial taxes at sale time. If you are reading this book because you are just beginning your transition planning, you should ask your tax advisor or an exit planning specialist about setting up the most favorable business structure for a sale.

Real Estate

Another issue in the sale of your business can be ownership of real property. Many business owners purchase a building for their company. Most often this asset is held outside of the corporate structure in another entity or in a family trust.

Sellers often start out with a specific idea of what they want to do with the real estate. Some want to lease it to the new owner for retirement income. For others, the equity in the real estate exceeds the equity in the company, and represents the majority of their proceeds at sale.

A building may create an asset base for the buyer to leverage in financing. SBA lenders, for example, will often finance a business over 10 years with 25% down, but will consider a building for 20 years and a 10% down payment. It is customary to see "blended" loans where the combined structure is something in between. For a buyer, the property's ability to extend the loan terms may make the difference between qualifying for financing and not.

On the other hand, the value of the building may put the total transaction beyond the buyer's ability to finance. He may want to relocate, or expand to a larger space. In such cases the real estate is a hindrance to a sale.

Real estate is often a critical part of company operations, as in a mobile home park or golf course. If you are acting as both landlord and tenant, however, you may find those roles in conflict when the time comes to sell. As in any business transaction, the odds of success are reduced in direct proportion to the preconditions you put on it.

I was asked to value a campground with some cabins recently. It was a beautiful setting; about 25 wooded acres that included a quarter mile of river bank. Only about a half hour from the city, it made an ideal getaway for locals, while offering travelers from a long distance a bucolic place to camp close to many tourist attractions.

The owners had run the business for over 40 years, and had many customers who came back year after year. Those customers had become friends, as had many other people in the small community in which the business was located.

Many other sections of the river had become centerpieces for high end residential developments. Those typically contained custom built 5,000 square foot plus homes on one acre lots, with shared access to river amenities and recreation.

I told the owners that based on their revenues and profits, the business had a value of about $1,000,000. They were highly offended, and accused me of trying to engineer a scam of some type. After all, a realtor had told them a few years before that the *land alone* was worth over $3,000,000.

After I calmed them down a bit, I explained that both the realtor and I were telling the truth. As the main asset of a small business, the land was worth a million dollars. As land alone, it was worth three times that. The business was not the best use of the asset from a profitability standpoint. In fact, it actually *decreased* the value of the property.

The owners were distraught. They had planned on getting three million dollars plus some more for the cabins, pool, and recreational facilities, in order to fund their retirement. They had already promised their customers and their friends in the community that they would only sell the campground as a business, and would not permit it to be developed as another residential subdivision.

Faced with a choice between eking out a living as elderly business owners and breaking their promises to friends, they chose the former. Their plan now is to run the business until they die, and let their heirs figure out what to do with it.

Be flexible. It's probably worth it to forego rental payments if the buyer wants to cash you out, just as it is to sell the building separately if he doesn't want to include it in the deal.

Asset Allocation (IRS Form 8594)

A seller typically wants as much of the sales price as possible classified as capital gain. **Unfortunately, some tax professionals are not fully up to speed on tax implications in a transaction environment.**

The Internal Revenue Service requires that an Asset Acquisition Statement (Form 8594) be filed with the transfer of a business. This form assigns values from the sale price to six classes of assets. Choices about this classification may engender very different levels of taxation.

The asset classes are:

Class I: Cash and cash equivalents

Class II: Securities and foreign currency

Class III: Debt instruments and accounts receivable

Class IV: Inventory and stock in trade

Class V: All assets not named in Classes I-IV, VI or VII. This generally means furniture, fixtures, equipment, rolling stock, and real estate;

Class VI: Intangible assets

Class VII: Goodwill

We'll discuss the last two classes of assets in a moment, but first a caution about the allocation for tangible assets, because there is a pitfall for sellers here as well.

It is customary to depreciate a tangible asset over its useful life, or some approximation of it. Once that asset is depreciated, it has no more value on the books, or in the eyes of the Internal Revenue Service.

Remember the example of the ten wheel drive Army surplus truck in Chapter 5? That asset had real value, but not according to the IRS. It was fully depreciated.

What happens if we list that truck on the Form 8594 as being $10,000 of the sale price? Many sellers assume that will be a capital gain. I sold an asset with a book value of zero for $10,000, so I will only owe capital gains tax on the profit.

Actually, it triggers what is called "depreciation recovery." What is depreciation recovery? It is the opinion of the IRS that since you fully depreciated the vehicle as having no value, and since it obviously *does* have value according to your own accounting for the sale price, you must then have previously taken an unjustified deduction from your income taxes. What does that mean? It means that you owe the IRS the taxes on $10,000 in prior income. Technically, you also owe the interest and penalties for as long as you've been "getting away" with the unjustified deduction.

On a $10,000 item, the difference is between 15% long term capital gains rate, and up to a 40% alternative minimum income tax rates (under present laws.) That is $2,500 in additional taxes.

On $500,000 worth of depreciated assets, the extra tax bite would be $125,000. And it gets worse. Since the money is owed for past periods, it is due *immediately*. If you are receiving it in installments, or took a note in payment, the IRS doesn't care. The tax is collectable right away.

I worked with a client who was buying lumber yards. He was negotiating for one where the family had written off substantial lumber inventory each year to avoid taxes.

One way to erase profits is to say that the asset is now worth less than what you paid for it. The reduction in value (or "shrink") is charged as an expense against profits in the current year. In inventory dependent businesses, this is sometimes sarcastically called the owner's invisible 401K. Inventory somehow manages to shrink each year just as much as is needed to absorb the taxable profits.

This practice had gone on for some time, and what looked like $2,000,000 of wood in the yard was on the books at about $800,000. Their local small-town CPA came up with a brilliant idea.

He told them to sell the inventory at $2,000,000, but to take back a ten year note in payment. He said that they would only owe capital gains tax on the portion of the note payments ($120,000 a year, or $18,000 tax) that exceeded the book value. Presto! The sale would yield a comfortable ten year retirement income of $182,000 a year after taxes.

I had to send the buyer back to the table to try and correct the mistake three times. The CPA grew increasingly insistent that he had "discovered" a brilliant tax strategy. Finally, my client told the CPA to show him the tax code that permitted such treatment of the gains. The CPA finally admitted that he was "a little vague on some of the more recent tax changes." At the next meeting he withdrew the structure, saying that tax codes changed all the time and no one could be expected to keep up with every detail.

That "recent" tax change was over 25 years old. Depreciation recovery is a frequent enough problem to go over again. When you write off an asset for taxes, the IRS assumes that you are taking a legitimate deduction. A sudden discovery that the asset is worth more than you claimed isn't a capital gain, it is an admission that you deducted more from your taxes than you should have. The IRS wants those taxes you avoided taxed at the rate it would have received on the profit. Moreover, they see it as money you should have paid already, and they want it *right now*.

What the CPA recommended would have resulted in ordinary income of $1,200,000 and a tax liability of approximately $480,000 to the seller on the day of close. The sellers would have owed the IRS almost $300,000 more than they received in the first year. It wasn't my client's fault, but you can bet he would have been affected by the litigation that was certain to follow.

Intangible Assets and Goodwill

There is some room for cooperation between buyer and seller in the Class VI area of intangible assets. These are too often overlooked in a smaller transaction. They may represent an opportunity for the seller to take some capital gains, while still giving the buyer a depreciable (15-year) asset.

Intangible assets recognized by the IRS on Form 8594 are:

- Workforce in place
- Business books and records
- Operating systems
- Information databases
- Formulas or know-how
- Customer-based intangibles
- Vendor-based intangibles
- Licenses and permits
- Covenants not to compete
- Franchises, trademarks or trade names

As you can see, there is ample room for interpretation of what these assets are.

Many business owners confuse "Goodwill" with good will. The latter is something that people have towards you. The former is a tax term defined as "The difference between the value of assets acquired and the price paid." It's that simple. Goodwill in transaction terms is "everything else."

The zero sum tax game rigged by the IRS puts buyers and sellers on opposite sides of the table when it's time to allocate the purchase price. Where the price is allocated should be part of the negotiations, not something left to the closing table before it is addressed.

Liability occurs when a buyer or seller reports the transaction on his individual tax return in a manner different from what was reported on the Form 8594. That can trigger an audit and penalties. Make certain that you and your buyer agree on the asset allocation, and sign the IRS form 8594 at the closing.

I can't emphasize this point enough. **Talk with a qualified CPA about the tax impact of the sale before you even begin the process.**

9. The Seventh Thing You Need to Know: Financing

Now we will discuss one of the great ironies of a business sale. **The buyer's best tool in obtaining the trust and cooperation of a lender is...you!**

The seller determines the attractiveness of the buyer's financing application in three ways. First, the seller is responsible for the cohesiveness and clarity of the financial information. Second, by his contributions to the seller's business plan, especially regarding details of profitability and plans for future growth. Finally, the seller provides credibility to the buyer by showing financial confidence in her.

Financial Data

Your financial information is the principle tool in creating the buyer's loan application. He or she will use your tax returns, your income statement and you balance sheet as the basis for his business plan. Copies of your asset lists, cost of goods analysis and overhead costs will be in the banker's hands, probably without any modification.

Remember the presentation tips that are covered in Chapter 7. It is human nature for anyone to give greater credence to exhibits that look professional, and lenders are human (regardless of your feelings about them!) Providing the buyer with clean, attractive support for his financing application makes everyone's job easier.

Once again, honesty in presenting the blemishes in your financial data is of paramount importance. Have you even played "telephone?" That's the game where you say something to the person next to you in a circle, and they pass it on to the next person until it comes back to you. If you have, you know that the final result seldom resembles the sentence you started with.

The same is true for verbal descriptions of business issues. Perhaps you have a business that is impacted by weather, and two years ago your area had the most rain in 100 years. In most years you just schedule around bad weather, but that year it rained for 104 days out of 120. You explain to the buyer why the record rainfall caused a dip in revenues that season.

The buyer tells the banker that revenues in the business can *occasionally* be impacted by bad weather. The banker tells the loan packaging officer (who is frequently a different person) that the business *depends* on weather conditions for its revenue. The packaging officer tells the loan committee that the *primary* factor in maintaining ongoing profitability is the number of sunny days in a year. The loan committee declines funding; because the business is too dependent on uncontrollable factors.

You will most likely not be at the buyer's side when he talks to his lender, and the buyer will not be there when the bank officer presents the loan for approval. Explain any special circumstances in writing, so that the story remains consistent all the way up the line.

Buyers are typically conservative in their approach to your company, but that conservative tendency is multiplied in the banker's approach to the deal. Just as a buyer usually wants to see more information than you are willing to provide at each stage of the process, a banker will frequently ask to see even more data in even greater detail. It is perfectly appropriate to ask the banker what his concerns are, and to offer information that only fits his needs. If, for instance, he wants to know what revenues are concentrated in your largest customers, hand him a summary of customers by size. Don't automatically assume that he needs to see all of your sales data.

Keep in mind that the buyer is the banker's customer. Since he is acting as an advisor to the buyer, he is perfectly within his rights to point out to the buyer anything that he sees as a flaw in your company. Most bankers take pride in their ability to spot issues, whether real or imagined. If it causes their client to renegotiate a lower price for the business, it simply makes the bank's loan security that much stronger.

Buyer Financing

There are three main sources of financing for a business purchase: the buyer's own investment capital, seller financing, and third party financing.

In most small business purchases the buyer seeks to put down 20% to 30% of the price from his personal savings. He or she then finances the rest from a combination of institutional and seller financing (see Chapters 9 and 10).

Any seller should carefully qualify buyers on the basis of their "bankability," whether or not you are considering financing part of the sale price. The financial strength of your buyer will determine your ability to sell your company.

Many buyers will begin the negotiation process by saying that they have little or no money to put down. It's true that few individuals approach a purchase of a Main Street business with a large hoard of cash for a down payment and working capital. Qualified buyers have other sources, however, if they are convinced that they need them. If you feel that you have a serious buyer, it is absolutely your right to ask detailed questions about how he or she will put enough of his or her own money into the deal to satisfy a lender.

Former corporate executives can tap their retirement savings without incurring a tax penalty for early withdrawal. There are a number of companies that specialize in converting 401K and IRA funds into self-directed funds. Some buyers don't know this, and others would prefer to keep that money as a hedge against failure. In any case, few will volunteer to tap those funds unless they believe that it is absolutely necessary to close an attractive deal.

Some buyers have personal lines of credit that they don't list on their financial statements. Others have substantial equity in a home or investment property. Still more can borrow capital from relatives. As any professional financier will tell you, if someone doesn't believe the risk is appropriate for friends or relatives, why should you or a bank be more comfortable than they are when it comes to lending on the deal?

Your first step in financial qualification of a buyer is to know how the down payment will be made. Some buyers will claim that they have investors ready to write a check. This is seldom the truth. They may have had a vague conversation with family about "help" in buying a business, or know someone who offered to assist them in getting started. This seldom translates into real cash at closing.

If a buyer claims that his funding will come from private investors, insist on qualifying those investors before moving forward in the negotiations. Frequently the buyer is surprised at what an investor considers a sizeable investment, or thinks that the investor is far wealthier than he really is. "Whatever you need" may be $50,000 in the buyer's mind, but $5,000 in the investor's. Like a banker, the investor is likely to be far more critical of the deal than the buyer.

"My investors prefer to remain anonymous," is a clear sign that you should disengage. I have never actually seen or heard of a deal closing with money that was hidden behind door number 3.

Another indication that you need to run for the hills is a buyer who says "I like to be creative. I don't have cash, but I can provide non-cash assets worth far more than what you are asking." Those non-cash assets always turn out to be something you won't want, can't use, or are highly overvalued. Tell that prospect that you prefer he sell the assets, pocket all that excess value, and just bring good old cash to the table.

Non-bank Lenders

A wide variety of players actively generate funds for small business purchases. Most of these are banking institutions, but there are also many non-bank lenders.

Financing for a purchase can sometimes be obtained from insurance companies, private equity groups, or other investors. Insurance companies are identical to any other portfolio investor. They prefer deals with substantial fixed assets like real estate, and with a long track record of stable returns.

Private Equity Groups (PEGs) actively purchase companies for investment returns. Most concentrate in a few industries, like printing or automotive, and bring substantial knowledge to the table about their areas of specialty. They will have very clear ideas about how much the company is worth, and can be tough negotiators. In most cases, but not all, they want a majority position, so the buyer with whom you are dealing could be replaced if the company doesn't perform. They also may want you to commit to staying active in the business for some time.

Private Equity Groups exploded during the first decade of the 21st century. Between 2000 and 2006 the market grew from 1,000 to over 7,000 firms, all seeking companies to buy. They were fueled by investors seeking higher returns than they could get in other markets. One estimate showed them raising over $500,000,000,000 in acquisition capital in 2008 alone.

Before you get too excited, however, PEGs are not an option for most Main Street sellers. Because they have both substantial overhead and require a high level of Return on Investment (ROI), they seek only companies that can provide excellent cash flow. The typical base line for a PEG to consider a prospective acquisition starts at about $1,000,000 in annual EBITDA.

Another available source of funds may be a vendor or supplier group. Some vendors will finance a purchase to maintain a customer or in return for a long term buying commitment. If your company is a critical piece of a large vendor's network, say one of the top five distributors or with exclusivity in an important market, you may wish to approach your vendor about financing an acquisition.

In franchising and captive distribution networks like branded insurance agencies it's common for the franchisor or exclusive vendor to have financing arrangements in place for business transfers. Those entities may help hundreds of businesses to sell each year, and can save you a lot of time qualifying buyers and closing the sale.

If you are seeking help from a vendor or franchisor, make contact with their corporate business development or franchise sales department. The local or regional operations or sales manager (frequently your best known point of contact) isn't qualified to discuss the sale of your business. Frequently those employees are a major risk for breaching confidentiality. They may seek personal benefit from the information, such as using it to help a favorite customer who is your competitor.

The U.S. Small Business Administration

The U.S. Small Business Administration (SBA) guarantees many small business acquisitions through participating lending institutions, but banks, asset-based lenders and private equity institutions also finance business acquisitions through conventional loans or more creative debt instruments.

Some lending institutions prefer SBA-guaranteed loans because their lending risk is reduced by SBA guarantees. Buyers like SBA loans because they tend to have much longer maturities than conventional financing: up to 25 years for real estate loans and up to 10 years for other business purposes. Longer maturities result in lower monthly debt service, making feasible many acquisitions that could not be done with shorter-term conventional financing.

The SBA places considerable emphasis on the buyer's experience in the industry and the asset base of the business.

SBA loans are more challenging to obtain for service businesses, or for others with few tangible assets.

The SBA has a number of programs for financing business purchases. Some are administered through Local Development Corporations (LDC) that are joint ventures with local governments. Other funding can be obtained through Small Business Investment Companies (SBIC), which act as direct investors in business enterprises.

The SBA isn't (at least at the time of publication) a direct lender to small businesses. They are a guarantor of loans made by others. The bank or other lender creates the loan, services it, and sets the terms (as long as they are at least to SBA standards.) The SBA assures the lender that at least 60% of the loan will be repaid. The lender's risk is thus reduced to the remaining 40% of the loan.

The SBA is a primary force in many small business loans, especially for a service business. **There are no collateral requirements for an SBA loan.** Many bankers will tell you that the security in a transaction doesn't meet SBA standards. This isn't true, since the SBA *has* no standards. What he is saying is that the security doesn't meet *his* bank's standards for SBA loans. It might meet another lender's requirements.

Although the SBA is a pure cash flow guarantor, using the SBA adds time to the approval process, and adds some fees to the closing costs. It is usually preferable to use a conventional lender if the deal will sustain the cash flow requirements; but many small business deals would never happen if it weren't for the SBA.

If the buyer is considering an SBA loan, or if you know your business model will require cash flow financing, investigate which lenders in your area are preferred SBA lenders. "Preferred" doesn't mean that they get special deals, but rather that the bank is permitted to make its own decisions about SBA-guaranteed loans as long as they remain within the guidelines.

Talk to the designated SBA loan officer in each bank. Like any lender, most have industries that they prefer and some that they won't touch regardless of how appealing the numbers look. I know SBA preferred lenders who will not look at a convenience store, while another in the same city funds dozens every year.

Just as they may like specific industries, some banks prefer to make acquisition loans, while others limit themselves to working capital loans for existing businesses. Trying to convince a working capital lender to fund an acquisition is a waste of time. Ask the bank loan officer to describe the number, average size and purpose of the bank's SBA deals before starting the application process.

There are a few SBA packagers around the country who know lenders' preferences and specialize in placing SBA loan applications where they are most likely to be approved. Their fees are usually modest. A good business intermediary can point you to one of these brokers.

Considerable information on loans and other small business issues is available at www.SBA.gov.

Loan Approval

Any lender will review both the business and the buyer. A strong buyer may be refused funding because the business is reporting declining trends. A good business may not be able to generate financing for a weak buyer. Lenders will depend heavily on the "Five C's" of credit, as outlined below.

Financial institutions will evaluate the attractiveness and feasibility of a business acquisition loan based on several factors:

- How comfortably the available cash flow from the business supports the service of the debt. Banks prefer that the historical (not the projected) cash flow of the business can support future debt by a ratio of at least 1.25 to 1.00.

- How predictable that projected cash flow is, as a function of recent performance, and the trend in sales and profits for the past three years

- The experience of the buyer in running businesses of the same nature

- The quality of the business plan presented by the buyer

- The five Cs of credit:

Character — What is the character of the buyer? What is his or her reputation in the industry and the community? This is one of the reasons why the credit scoring process evolved, with a large component being your personal credit history.

Capacity — How much debt can the company handle? Will the buyer be able to honor the obligation and repay the debt? There are numerous financial benchmarks, such as debt and liquidity ratios, that banks evaluate before advancing funds.

Capital — How well capitalized is the company? How much money is the buyer investing in the business? Lenders want to see that the buyer has a financial commitment, and has put himself at risk in the company. Both your company's financial statements and his personal credit are keys to the capital question.

Conditions — What are the current economic conditions and how is your company impacted? If your business is sensitive to economic downturns, for example, the bank wants a comfort level that the buyer can manage varying levels of productivity and expenses. Are there any economic or political issues on the horizon that could negatively impact the growth of the business?

Collateral — While cash flow will nearly always be the primary source of repayment of a loan, bankers look at what they call the secondary sources of repayment. Collateral represents assets that are pledged as an alternate repayment source for the loan. Most collateral is in the form of hard assets, such as real estate and office or manufacturing equipment. Additionally, your accounts receivable and inventory may be pledged as collateral, although at a discount to their book value.

Collateral typically includes some or all of the buyer's personal assets. He or she will be asked to sign a general personal guarantee. Frequently, the buyer is asked to pledge the equity in a home.

The bank is also motivated to see the business transfer free of liens and debt (see Chapter 5). The more that other claims against the business can be eliminated, the more the bank's position is secured.

In most business acquisition lending there are a couple more "C's" that apply to the <u>seller</u>; Confidence and Commitment. The lender wants to see a sign of the seller's confidence in the buyer. This is frequently in the form of a portion of the purchase price being contingent on the buyer's success. I'll discuss this more in the next chapter.

The lender also wants to see the seller's commitment. Is he staying around for a reasonable time after the sale? Does the buyer have recourse (other than litigation) if things aren't all as they are supposed to be? Will the seller return, or offer consulting help if the buyer is struggling?

Your attitude towards the buyer has an influence on the lender. If you take the position that you want to get as far away as possible immediately following the closing, or you want every penny in your pocket on the day the deal is done, expect the lender to become far more cautious.

10. The Eighth Thing You Need to Know: Seller Notes

Seller financing is so common in small business transactions that it needs a chapter to itself. You may take a note for a portion of the sale, finance part of the down payment to help the buyer qualify for a loan, or receive some of the value of the business contingent on future performance. Regardless of the methodology, in the majority of Main Street business sales to individual buyers the seller will represent part of the financing package.

Financing the Entire Sale

Some business brokers insist on 100% seller financing as a pre-condition of any listing. That's just an indication of a lazy broker. Seller financing is simple, quick, and attractive, but there is no reason it should be used when more conventional financing options are available.

There are some businesses that can't be sold unless the seller finances the sale. The most frequent situation in which this is the case is with an unprofitable company or one that has closed. If there are no profits, it is tough to convince a lender to fund even at asset value. There may be no choice but for the seller to take a note.

Seller financing is also common in very small transactions. Sometimes a small loan is harder to place than a large one. If the buyer needs less than $100,000 to close the purchase, both parties may be better off if the seller just holds the note.

Seller financing is fast. In the case of an owner's death or disability, the family may have to dispose of the business in a very short time. Seller financing may be the only way to get a new owner in place quickly enough to save the business.

If you have a highly qualified buyer, seller financing may be your preferred option. Say your company is being purchased by another business. The buyer is substantial, can guarantee the note, and is willing to pay over time. Holding the note yourself can yield a steady cash flow for several years, plus the benefit of interest income.

Similarly, there are many instances in which seller financing can be used to defer taxes. You may want to consider holding a note simply to reduce your immediate tax liability.

Perhaps the most important factor influencing a seller's decision to finance is price. You want to leave your business. The buyer can't make the numbers add up to something on which a bank will lend. Should you choose to close your company? In reality, seller financing allows you to continue receiving the profits of your company after you have stopped working in it.

Frequently seller financing represents a tactic to permit a higher selling price for the company. How many people would buy expensive cars if they had to pay cash on the day they drove off?

Seller financing becomes the equivalent of "EZ payment terms" in auto sales. If you can make the purchase more affordable to the buyer, you will qualify more potential buyers and can demand a higher price.

Collateral and Security

Seller financing is also a way to "keep your eye on the store." If you have built up great relations with employees or customers, for example, you may feel obligated to make certain that they get a fair shake going forward.

Make no mistake. If you take a note back on the purchase of your business, you will be a partner in the business until you are fully paid. The terms of a seller note should contain your right to examine the books and inspect the operations for as long as you are a creditor.

The most common remedy for default on your note is the right to take back control of your business. In many cases the need for seller financing means that the buyer can't or won't use other assets for security. If the buyer had substantial outside equity, seller financing would probably have been less likely.

If your only recourse is to reclaim the business, make sure that the terms are flexible enough to let you move before the business is ruined, and that you pay careful attention to current circumstances. Many sellers have moved to repossess their business too late, and found a company that is worth a fraction of the one that was originally sold.

Earn-outs

Sometimes seller financing is in the form of earn-outs, or payments conditioned on the performance of the business after closing. This method of financing makes sense in a number of situations.

You may take an earn-out because you don't want to discount the business based on its most recent performance. This would be the case if your company is experiencing a temporary dip in sales or profits, but conditions are otherwise favorable for your exit. Therefore, you might make part of the purchase price conditional on the business recovering to its previous levels.

Similarly, you may have recently made a major investment in new equipment, just signed an agreement with a big new customer, or invested in new advertising that hasn't hit the marketplace yet. You would want an earn-out based on improved sales or profits, so that you could realize some of the return on your investment.

Sometimes the company has been growing rapidly. You may be selling for other reasons, but feel that you've built a foundation that has lots of momentum.

Finally, you may have buyers who are concerned that the company will collapse without you, and you want to give them some comfort that won't be the case. This is the most frequent reason for negotiating an earn-out in a small business.

Earn-outs are also used in distress sales when the seller has little room to negotiate. Sometimes the only way to realize <u>any</u> money for the business is to get conditional payments based on future business.

Whatever the reason for an earn-out, you need the same rights to look at the books and watch the operations as in any other type of seller financing. Make sure any agreement specifies your right to keep an eye on the business.

Lender Demands for Seller Financing

Many lenders (including the SBA) see seller financing as equivalent to buyer equity in a deal, and as an insurance policy against seller fraud.

Having the seller take some of the purchase price as a note improves the ratio of bank debt to owner's equity in the transaction. Ironically, a bank may lend more money to a buyer who has the additional debt of seller financing than they would to one who doesn't.

Not surprisingly, the lenders may regard your willingness to hold some debt on the sale as a vote of confidence in the buyer. They also assume that you have a vested interest in making the new owner successful, since his ability to generate profit is a prerequisite to you receiving your full selling price.

Seller financing is usually subordinated to any other third party financing. Quite simply, subordination means that the bank gets paid first. In the event of a default, the lender's position is ahead of yours. If cash flow is close to the minimum acceptable for loan approval, the lender may require that the seller's note pay you interest only for the first few years, and may sometimes dictate no payments at all until cash flow improves.

Seller notes may also have restrictions on payment unless certain requirements, known as covenants, are met to assure the other lenders of the security of their debt. Common covenants include minimum levels of inventory, cash on hand, or accounts receivable.

Why would a seller agree to all these restrictions? It's simple-without them the bank won't finance the deal, and the seller would have to carry all the risk. Faced with a choice between selling the business and not selling it; or between walking away with most of the cash against getting only a note, most sellers will choose to satisfy the bank's demands.

Whose Money is It?

The most frequent objection to seller financing is: **"If the buyer uses my profits to pay me over time, I am paying for the purchase of my own business!"** It can be aggravating to structure a deal that conserves cash for the buyer, and forces you to continue sharing the risk after you no longer own the business.

If you are the founder of the company, you probably remember some lean days at the beginning. You took the risks of starting a business. Now a buyer and his lender are saying that he shouldn't have to bear the same risks. You didn't struggle to build a business so that someone else could have an easy job of running it!

Remember, **any form of a business sale is simply a way to realize future earnings of your business without having to do the work yourself.** Your buyer will work for years to come to earn the money he is borrowing to pay you. It will all seem more reasonable when you check your bank balance from the laptop on the porch of your beach house.

11. The Ninth Thing You Need to Know: Business Brokers

Four out of five Main Street businesses listed on the market are for sale by the owner (FSBO). Four out of five businesses on the market <u>never get sold</u>. That doesn't mean that FSBOs never sell, or that businesses represented by brokers always sell. They don't. But there must be some correlation between the low percentage of businesses for sale that are represented by professionals, and the low percentage that are actually sold.

What happens to the rest of the businesses? Many simply close. Frequently, putting a business up for sale is merely a last gasp attempt to salvage something from a rapidly deteriorating situation. Remember the Dismal Ds in Chapter 5?

Selling your business is probably the single most important financial event of your life. You wouldn't dream of representing yourself in a lawsuit, or completing a complex tax return without the help of a CPA. Why then do so many business owners feel that they can sell their business without the help of a professional?

I think that there are three likely reasons why the majority of business owners don't hire a broker to sell their business. First, they think that because they know their business better than anyone, they are the best equipped person to sell it. Second, many businesses are really not saleable, and the owner frequently suspects as much. Third, the level of professionalism of many business brokers fails to create much confidence in their prospective customers.

"I'll sell it myself."

Let's look at the "I know my business best" argument. This is frequently accompanied by such supporting comments as "A broker won't know what is important to tell people" and "I'm going to have to make all the decisions in negotiations anyway." There's some truth to all those statements.

If you are involved in litigation, what do you expect from the attorney? He obviously doesn't know the circumstances of the lawsuit. He learns them from you. He doesn't make the decisions. You are the client, and you will determine whether an offer or settlement is acceptable to you.

The attorney helps you to analyze the facts of your case, and uses his experience to suggest the points that should be emphasized or downplayed. He organizes your materials and puts them in an order that is understandable to others (a judge or jury). He anticipates what the other party will do, based on his knowledge of how others in similar situations have behaved.

All of these are similar (actually, identical) to the skills and contributions of a good business broker. A good broker provides the following in a sale:

- <u>Access</u> to multiple avenues and methodologies for marketing your business

- <u>Confidentiality</u>: Brokers don't put a "for sale" sign on your front sidewalk. That can upset employees, vendors and customers. How would you interact with prospective buyers without revealing who you are?

- <u>Objectivity</u>: Selling and buying are both emotional decisions. The broker doesn't have your visceral attachment to the company.

- <u>Familiarity</u> with the process. What do you do when a buyer asks for more information? How do you counter a buyer's claim of reduced value? A broker has seen and heard these questions before, and should know both the appropriate responses and the techniques for delivering them.

- <u>Positioning</u>: The broker can help you to present the company in the best light, and target the right buyers.

- • <u>Distraction</u>: The sale process is time and attention consuming. Many owners have let the company slide while engaged in negotiations, and them seen the buyer reduce the price or walk away.

Brokers typically work in specific segments, or strata of the marketplace. Choose one who fits with the business that you are trying to sell. The term "business broker" typically refers to those who handle Main Street transactions. Those are the businesses where the buyer is seeking to make a livelihood from the company that he or she acquires. Larger sales are more often handled by investment bankers or Merger and Acquisition professionals.

Qualifying a Broker

As with any other professional, a broker should be selected on the basis of professionalism and integrity. How can a seller judge these factors? Here are some questions that should be asked as part of your research:

- • How will you go about selling my business?
- • What is your experience in selling businesses?
- • What professional certifications do you have?
- • How much do you know about my industry?
- • How will you find buyers for my business?
- • Do you have any sources of buyers other than those responding to advertisements?
- • How effectively can you help buyers obtain financing?
- • Can you provide references whom I can contact directly?
- • How will you advertise and market my business?
- • What web sites do you utilize?
- • How often will you report to me on activity, and on your follow-up of prospects?
- • Do you charge up-front fees?
- • What help do you provide in preparing financial documents for a buyer's review?

- Will you accompany buyers on all site visits?
- Will you act as an intermediary in the negotiations?
- Can I see an example of your presentation materials for another listing?

Business Brokerage became recognized as a profession in the mid-1970's. Because it is a relatively new and unregulated profession, other professionals regularly claim to be brokers in addition to their normal practice. Accountants have extensive financial expertise, attorneys possess contract knowledge, and real estate brokers have transaction experience. Business brokerage, however, requires knowledge, education, and experience in all three of those disciplines, plus additional abilities in marketing, advertising, and negotiations.

The premier professional association in the industry is the International Business Brokers Association (IBBA). The IBBA provides certification of brokers. The Certified Business Intermediary (CBI) requires 68 hours of education in the field, attendance at a minimum of one International Conference, and adherence to the IBBA code of ethics. To maintain the certification requires continued attendance at educational conferences plus about 18 hours of additional course work annually.

Regulation of business brokers varies widely from state to state. Some are required to have real estate licenses. Some have special brokerage licenses. Some states require both, others require none. In some states, brokers are the seller's fiduciary, meaning that they have an obligation to serve the client's interest before their own. In others, they represent either buyer or seller, depending on their role in the transaction. You should know what the legal status of a broker is before you agree to representation.

Sellers should exercise special care with brokers who make unsubstantiated claims. Several large "business brokers" who operate nationally actually get over 90% of their income from their fees for *listing* the companies for sale. Less than 10% is commission from actually *selling* companies. Some organizations make claims about having "secret" buyers in Europe and Asia, or strategic buyers who purchase only through them, and pay far more than market prices. When asked for references, they frequently say that the information is too "sensitive" to share.

Qualified buyers in other countries use the same lawyers and accountants as those in the USA. Those buyers didn't become wealthy by being ignorant. Similarly, large strategic buyers have personnel dedicated to acquisitions. They seldom limit themselves to an exclusive relationship with one organization. While finding a strategic acquirer can be a challenge, if your business is right for such a deal there are any number of investment bankers qualified to do the search for you. Investment bankers who focus on mid-market transactions (upwards of $3,000,000 sale price) usually get higher retainers and lower contingency percentages than business brokers.

When choosing a broker, check out the quality of his or her marketing materials. I am embarrassed to admit that many business brokers are astonishingly sloppy in their presentation of a business. I regularly see listings with typographical errors, misspellings, and erroneous information. Financial data is incomplete or simply added incorrectly. Copies are crooked, stained, or unreadable. Ask yourself if this is the way you want your business to be perceived. Many fine companies miss buyers because the information from the broker makes them look bad.

On a similar note, observe the quality of the information for the broker's other listings. If his other companies don't have comprehensive financials, current tax returns, and strong supporting documentation, the broker is unlikely to make a good case for your well-run company.

You should also look at the asking price for the broker's other listings. Is he or she representing companies whom you would consider peers in business? If the broker is dealing with buyers of $50,000 businesses all day, does he have the talent and resources to deal with buyers who are ready to spend $500,000 or $5,000,000?

Some sellers will choose a broker because he represents companies that are much larger and more profitable than theirs. In such cases, that broker may not be likely to spend as much time and energy marketing the smaller listings in his portfolio.

Becoming more knowledgeable about the process of selling a business will allow you to make a better hiring decision. I recommend extensive due diligence on the business broker's background, reputation, and business experience.

Ask for referrals from both sellers and those who have bought companies through the broker. A buyer will give you a better idea of how the broker acted with prospects. You may be surprised at how often I hear "I bought this business despite the broker, not because of him."

If you choose to hire a broker, it may be one of the most important business relationships you will ever form. The process of screening for the right professional can have a major impact on the success of your sale.

Broker Fees

The vast majority of Main Street business brokers work largely or entirely on contingency fees. That means that they only get paid if they sell your business. Many will ask for a nominal payment up front. This is acceptable, as it both defrays their expense in preparing the listing and qualifies the seller as serious about pursuing the transaction. These retainers are usually applied to any contingency fee when the deal closes.

The typical fee for a broker is 10% of the selling price for businesses selling at less than $1,000,000. For much smaller businesses there will frequently be a minimum fee, or a somewhat higher percentage.

Transactions larger than $2,000,000 are usually handled on a sliding scale of commissions. In Main Street brokerage, the most common formula is the "Double Lehman," named after the now-defunct Wall Street banking house. That formula is 10% of the first million dollars, 8% of the second million, 6% of the third, 4% of the fourth million, and 2% of anything in excess of $5,000,000. The use and forms of this formula vary, and it is important to document the levels and percentages up front.

Be aware that the selling price as described in a broker's listing agreement is typically all-encompassing. It includes any remuneration received for assets, assumption of debt, non-compete or consulting agreements, continued salary or benefits for the seller, royalties, lease payments, and personal property (such as a vehicle) taken in the sale. If you have things that you feel are simply *yours*, and don't intend to pay a broker for them, you should discuss that with him or her up front.

Many of these all-encompassing contract descriptions of a sale also include the current assets you will take from the business. Personally, I don't agree that retaining your working capital and accounts receivable, which are the result of your prior business activity, should be considered as part of the sale price. In many businesses, 10% of the collected cash represents more than the net profit you made. Also, your ability to take those assets with you is a standard practice, not the result of the broker's negotiations. I suggest negotiating to have those removed from any calculation of commissions.

Exclusivity and Co-brokerage

Most business broker listing agreements are exclusive. That means that you are not permitted to negotiate or sell to anyone except through the broker. In fact, exclusivity is a requirement under the IBBA code of ethics.

Many sellers want to list with several nonexclusive brokers. They feel that since all of them are working on a contingency basis, having competition will cause each broker to work harder. What would make exclusivity so important in protecting the client that the IBBA would include it in its code of ethics?

Imagine a scenario in which you had three brokers trying to sell your business, and all three had a prospective buyer. Each only makes a commission if <u>his</u> buyer succeeds. Whom do you think he represents? Each broker's financial interest becomes selling <u>you</u> on the desirability of his buyer; not the other way around. Competing brokers have an innate conflict of interest. It is important enough that I would <u>not</u> recommend hiring any broker who is willing to take a listing on a non-exclusive basis.

As the seller, how would you compare offers? Did all buyers get the same information? Was the qualification process for each the same? Do they all have the same chance at financing? Exclusivity simply takes one large component, that of conflicting broker self-interest, out of the equation.

Remember, exclusivity means that the broker is compensated even if you find the buyer yourself. If you think that the most likely buyer for your business is a friend, relative, employee, competitor or vendor, consider hiring a broker or exit planner in more of a consulting role just to assist you in the transaction.

Although the broker is obliged as your agent to represent your interests above his or her own, most do not see that as extending to their commission. Business brokers do not typically employ a Multiple Listing Service like realtors do. In an exclusive listing, the broker has a choice of cooperating with another broker. Many brokers flatly refuse to engage in co-brokerage.

There are some legitimate reasons not to co-broker. The broker may not feel that another broker is sufficiently professional, or that the buyer is qualified. There are few good reasons (other than greed) however, to have a blanket policy against co-brokerage. Ask the broker up front what his policy is on co-brokering, and why.

Buyer Representatives

If you are a business owner, you probably receive letters from business brokers saying that they have buyers looking for a business just like yours. Usually this is stretching the truth a bit. They *may* have buyers who are looking for good businesses, and yours *might* be one of them.

In most states (but not all), a broker is the representative of the person or entity who is paying his fee. Most brokers, therefore, are sellers' representatives, because the seller is paying the commission on a sale.

Some business brokers act as buyers' representatives. They are paid a retainer by the buyer for their work in searching out a suitable acquisition opportunity. In some cases, they are also paid a contingency fee for closing a transaction.

Buyer representation is most often associated with mid-market transactions. Private equity groups and publicly traded companies will retain acquisition specialists to locate viable merger targets on their behalf. True buyer representation is less frequently seen in Main Street brokerage.

Main Street deals are usually too small to bear the added cost of two broker fees. If a buyer is paying $300,000 for a company, for example, he is likely to make a $60,000 down payment. Typically, ten percent of the purchase price ($30,000) is paid to the selling broker out of that down payment. If the buyer had to pay another 5% to a buyer's broker, he would be adding 25% to his cash needs at close. Main Street buyers simply do not have the resources to add that kind of expense to a small company acquisition.

When you receive a "We have buyers!" letter, it seldom means that the broker has someone who has agreed to pay his fees. **Most Brokers expect the seller to sign a listing agreement and pay the full commission at close.**

Of course, as soon as you sign a listing agreement, the broker becomes <u>your</u> agent. That doesn't prevent some brokers from signing exclusive representation agreements with buyers that state they will receive their compensation from the seller. I've never understood how this works legally, but it occurs from time to time.

Generally, the "We have buyers!" marketing approach is harmless, even if it is a slight over statement. It has become so common that I think most owners have figured it out.

12. The Tenth Thing You Need to Know: Doing the Deal

Sellers will frequently ask me, **"How much do I have to pay to you if I find my own buyer?** All you need to do then is handle the paperwork."

Marketing to buyers is actually the easier part of a broker's job. The "paperwork" is at least half the work in any transaction, and sometimes a lot more.

Brokers enjoy economies of scale in the marketing of companies. The assembly of your documentation, preparation of listings, and talking to buyers is fairly straightforward, and is something they do every day. Once a buyer is ready to make an offer, the individualized effort of negotiating and structuring your deal and seeing it through to close begins.

Managing the Closing Process

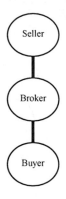

Managing the *sale* process is a time consuming business. If you have chosen to use an intermediary, such as a business broker or other qualified professional, he or she has been responsible for the majority of contacts with buyers. When a letter of intent is signed the intermediary becomes a coach, a coordinator, a drill sergeant, a negotiator and a file clerk all rolled into one. Someone has to deal with all the stakeholders in the business.

Managing the *closing* process looks more like this:

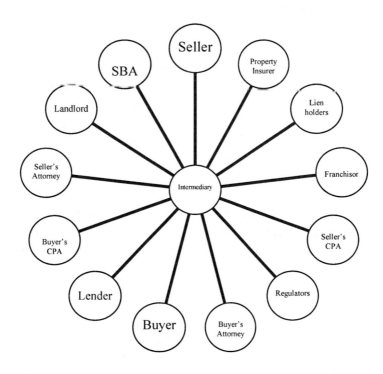

Each of the stakeholders shown in the diagram above may have some role in the selling of your business. Even if your transaction doesn't involve the SBA or a franchisor, there are many others who may have a legal right of approval over a change of ownership.

Do you have contracts with vendors that specify exclusive rights to sell a product, or a specific service territory? Those contracts often include their right to approve a change in ownership. If you supply certain customers, especially governmental entities, a change in ownership may trigger a new bid process.

If you have handled the sales process by yourself up to this point, it may be time to consider paying someone to help you coordinate the closing process. A qualified professional not only saves you time, he or she may save the deal. Many sellers have been distracted by the amount of effort it takes to close a transaction. They reduce their focus on the day-to-day operation of the business, and are shocked when the buyer wants to renegotiate the price because the business is declining.

Most importantly, **time is the enemy of all transactions**. Coordinating the stakeholders in a sale takes weeks at best, and can extend indefinitely at worst. In one transaction I brokered, the environmental regulators held up the closing for *three years*. The expensive soil remediation that was required wasn't unexpected, but the attorneys negotiated what the requirements were with the state inspector. Then the seller took a long time to get bids and decide on a contractor. By the time the remedial work was finally done, the state inspector involved had retired, and the new inspector demanded a completely different approach to resolving the issues. The deal eventually closed, but there were any number of times that we had almost given up on it.

There seems to be a variant of Murphy's Law at work when it comes to closing a business sale. The closer you get to being done, the more reasons there are to delay it. An attorney has a scheduled vacation. Your CPA is facing a tax filing deadline that consumes all of his resources. The lender wants to see just one more piece of information. The insurance policy is up for renewal. Getting all the players to the finish line simultaneously is sometimes a coordination task of Herculean proportions.

Letters of Intent

The sale transaction solidifies through a series of agreements and milestones. You started out with a Confidentiality or Non-Disclosure agreement with the buyer. Once he or she has decided to buy your business, the next step is to outline the general terms and conditions in a Letter of Intent (LOI.) Sometimes the Letter of Intent is very simple, with the deal parameters spelled out in an attached Term Sheet. For our purposes we'll call both forms a Letter of Intent.

Letters of Intent can be either binding or non-binding. Most Main Street business sales start with a non-binding letter of intent. In this, the buyer outlines the terms and conditions under which he is willing to purchase the business. Major components of a typical LOI include:

- The price to be paid

- Cash down payment

- Financing required, either from a third-party lender, the seller, or both

- The amount of time after close that the seller is expected to stay in the company, and whether that will be compensated.

- General provisions of a non-compete agreement

- Escrow money to be deposited upon acceptance

- Condition of the business at close, such as:
  - o Inventory levels
  - o Debt
  - o Retention of key employees
  - o Work in process
  - o Backlog

- Contingencies to closing, such as:
  - o Approval of financing
  - o Due Diligence
  - o Transfer of contracts
  - o Definitive purchase agreement(s)
  - o Leases

- Time frames and deadlines

Many sellers ask "Why, if so many factors are included in a Letter of Intent, isn't it binding?" The LOI is a general documentation of intent and conditions. It doesn't include the legal parameters, performance obligations, and a dozen other things that will come in the definitive purchase agreements. Ask yourself whether you would like to be in a position of litigating the most important financial event of your life based on a one or two page informal document? Except in the simplest of deals, the answer is "Probably not."

Definitive Purchase Agreements

The LOI is a framework for the attorneys to begin drafting the definitive agreements. These usually include an asset purchase agreement, the non-compete agreements and accompanying bills of sale or transfer agreements. Many small business owners have a healthy distaste for attorneys and their accompanying fees, but now is one of those times when you really need one. Make certain that your attorney is <u>qualified</u> to handle a business sale transaction (See Chapter 12).

Of course, the more detail there is in the LOI, the better a guideline it becomes for the attorneys. Make your wishes and intent plain in the LOI. Don't depend on your lawyer to figure it out for you.

Drafting the initial purchase agreement has to start someplace, and this is often another question to negotiate. Often, each party wants his attorney to draft the initial agreement. Regardless of how the document is started, there is a pitfall in having two attorneys working out the terms.

The American humorist Will Rogers once noted, "When I go through a small town, and they have one attorney, he is typically a man of fairly modest means. But when they have *two* attorneys, I notice that they are *both* doing real well."

In fairness, your attorney's job is to protect you. The buyer's attorney has the same responsibility. Failing to protect the client fully can leave a lawyer open to charges of malpractice. Any attorney's biggest fear is of making a mistake.

The problem usually begins when one party in the transaction gives the LOI to his attorney, saying "I want you to draft the purchase agreement for this deal, *and make sure that it protects me fully.*" The attorney is now under an obligation to put into the agreement everything his education, training and experience have taught him about protecting the client. "Everything" frequently makes a two page LOI into a 30 page purchase contract.

Under these circumstances, your attorney is not obliged to be reasonable, fair, or to worry about the impact of his work on the success of the transaction. He is obligated only to protect you first, and himself second. The contract can be, and usually is, completely one-sided in your favor.

Now, let's bring in the second attorney. You (or the buyer, depending on who went first) give similar instructions. The second attorney deletes all the one-sided language, and replaces it with one-sided language protecting <u>his</u> client to the detriment of the other. Your 30 page document now has 20 pages of revisions, most of which the first attorney will refuse to accept.

Do you understand why Will Rogers' two attorneys both thrive? The problem isn't necessarily greed (although that sometimes enters into it,) but the lawyers' need to create a paper trail that shows that they at least *tried* to do everything that they could think of. This way, if there is later litigation over the terms of the agreement, they can point to earlier versions that show how they attempted to protect their clients.

That's why attorneys are called "deal killers." It isn't because they are opposed to letting contracts go forward, but the process and the system frequently require that they put roadblocks in its path.

I've seen two parties in a $120,000 sale of a pizzeria run up over $30,000 in legal fees this way.

I often recommend in Main Street transactions that the two parties jointly hire an attorney to draft agreements on behalf of the transaction. This attorney doesn't represent either party, but instead tries to craft a balanced agreement. Then each party uses his or her own lawyer to review the documents. Starting with a balanced agreement, which both clients say meets their general intentions, greatly reduces the lawyers need to add protective language. Ironically, having three attorneys in a deal frequently costs less than having two. Unfortunately, some state Bar Associations forbid such an approach. (Gee…I wonder why?)

The biggest area for negotiation in the definitive agreement revolves around representations, warranties and indemnification. This is where the buyer and seller document the conditions of the business and claims made about it, along with the penalties they will be subject to if those conditions or claims turn out to be different.

Be careful of warranties and indemnifications that extend past closing. Some, like subjecting inventory to physical verification, are reasonable. Others, like allowing unlimited offset of the seller's note for repairs, are not. These two examples by themselves illustrate why a simple LOI is not enough to transfer ownership.

The Definitive Agreement process is also the appropriate time to fill in the IRS form 8594 for purchase price allocation (see Chapter 8).

Contingencies and Conditions to Close

The Letter of Intent should have spelled out contingencies and conditions to closing. Part of the management process in any closing is creating a checklist of these items, and crossing them off as they are fulfilled.

In many transactions, it is wise to have a series of sign-off agreements for the buyer to document that each contingency has been completed to his satisfaction.

The biggest condition is usually due diligence. Due diligence is the process by which the buyer confirms the facts of the business as presented by the seller. Are the contracts current? Are the business processes documented? Does all the equipment work? Is the inventory really there?

Frankly, if a buyer has lost his enthusiasm for the deal, there is almost always a way for him to back out by deciding that you failed the due diligence process. That's why having clean and organized documentation is vital. Remember, time is your enemy. The longer the due diligence process lasts, the more things the buyer will think up to be worried about.

Some items are conditions to closing. This means that their confirmation requires more than just checking. The two most frequently occurring examples of major conditions are favorable outcomes of discussions with key customers and meetings with key employees.

Clearly, you don't want a prospective buyer talking to key customers or employees until the deal is a near certainty. At the earliest, these conversations should be conditioned upon approval of financing by a third party lender. Many times, the key employee conversations are held with both buyer and seller in attendance on the morning of closing.

Here is a cautionary note about informing key employees. If the business really can't function without them (or at least they think it can't) they could decide that some portion of the proceeds is rightfully theirs. I know of one case in which the buyers in a $10,000,000 transaction told the Operations Manager "We are so glad you are part of this company. We wouldn't be spending $10,000,000 on this if you weren't here."

The manager was in the owner's office five minutes after the buyers left. It cost the owner a hefty six figure bonus to buy the manager's agreement to stay. Consider structuring a past-closing stay agreement with key employees before putting the company up for sale. It is usually a lot more expensive once they know that their participation is critical.

On the other hand, I know one business owner who has made seven acquisitions in the printing and mailing industry. His policy is to close the transaction without talking to any employees or customers in advance. He drives from the closing at the attorney's office to the business, accompanied by the former owner. They call all the employees together, usually out on the shop floor, and he makes the following very short speech.

"I have just purchased this business from Bob. I own a number of similar companies, and we think that adding yours will give you greater opportunities and room for growth. Otherwise, we will be operating much as you have all along. Thank you, and now please return to work."

He has never had an employee protest or quit. Inertia and familiarity can be powerful forces.

13. The Eleventh Thing You Need to Know: The Roles of Professionals

The role of attorneys, CPAs, and other business advisors in a business sale is crucial, but even highly experienced professionals must be properly managed. While many are experts in areas of finance and law, **not all financial and legal professionals are familiar with the process of selling a business.**

If you had a pain in your chest, would you go to a podiatrist? That sounds silly, because the difference is so obvious. But what if you had a pain in your wrist? Would you go to an orthopedic surgeon, or a neurologist, or a physical therapist, or an internist just to get some painkillers? Each is a trained professional. Each treats wrist pain; but if your problem is neurological, three of the four aren't qualified to help you, and could possibly do more damage.

The analogy works just as well in the sale of a business. All Certified Public Accountants understand financial statements and tax returns. All attorneys comprehend contracts. But that doesn't mean that all are equally qualified to handle the sale of a business.

One of the worst closings I had was when the buyer insisted, absolutely insisted, that his family attorney, an estate planning specialist, had to handle the deal. The seller for his side used a good friend, one of the top business litigators in the area.

The estate attorney almost blew up the deal multiple times by sticking in cute little devices to save his client a few dollars in taxes. The fact that each little change (which was neither discussed with the client nor with the other attorney) cost the seller an equal amount of *additional* taxes seemed to escape him. Every time he sent a contract back it had some new thing buried in it to favor the buyer and hurt the seller. He completely destroyed any trust in the negotiations.

The seller's attorney was worse. He had won many big judgments in the courtroom by finding one little error or slip in a deal, and he was determined not to let his seller friend fall prey to any such mistake. He papered each aspect of the deal with separate agreements, running to a couple of hundred pages in total. All this for a $200,000 sale!

Even worse, he insisted that every document be clearly drafted and dated as of the day of close. He would not permit any manual corrections. Unfortunately, the SBA kept delaying the funding by a day or two. Every 48 hours, the documentation had to be re-dated and reprinted...six sets of almost 150 pages each!

Damaging Your Interests

Some CPAs and attorneys feel a need to justify their fees by showing financial savings as a direct result of their work. They try to tell the client that they have "improved" the deal on the client's behalf. Unfortunately, these efforts often hurt the deal rather than move it towards a speedy close.

In one recent small business sale that we handled, both parties sent the purchase agreement to their attorneys for review. The buyer's attorney rewrote the terms of the note at a lower interest rate, and inserted a clause requiring the buyer to pay for some asset improvements after the sale.

The seller's attorney rewrote the terms of the note at a higher interest rate, and restructured the asset bill of sale to shift the entire tax burden to the buyer.

The terms of the note had been previously agreed between buyer and seller during the negotiations. Neither attorney asked his client whether he wanted the changes made. Both attorneys were paid a second time to review the agreement again after the original terms were restored.

Similarly, a CPA who is inexperienced in transaction work may advise his client to change the purchase price allocation to qualify for better tax treatment. For some reason, the accountant doesn't seem to realize that there is another party to the deal, and the structure might be as it is for a very good reason. Some CPAs have become so fixated on their quest for tax avoidance that common sense seems to elude them.

Unfortunately, the other party in the deal frequently perceives such changes as dishonest attempts to gain advantage in the sale. Weeks or months of careful negotiation and trust can be blown out of the water by a careless or naïve advisor.

Attorneys, accountants, and other advisors who are experienced in small business transfers will expedite the deal, not slow it down. They will help you to avoid pitfalls, not create them.

Qualifying professionals can be challenging. Most friends will happily refer you to a "good lawyer" or a "smart accountant." That doesn't necessarily mean that they understand business sales, although many will claim to have sufficient related experience.

I can tell you from my own experience; a real estate attorney might have hundreds of property sales under his belt, and still know next to nothing about business transfers. Similarly, just because a CPA has prepared hundreds of small business tax returns doesn't necessarily qualify her to advise about the tax implications in a business sale.

There is one more caution I have to offer about choosing professionals. **The most important single financial event of your life, the sale of your business, isn't the time to save a few hundred dollars on advice.** Paying high fees doesn't, by itself, guarantee competence. But hiring the cheapest advisors you can find can cost you many times the money you might save.

The first question to any prospective professional advisor is "What is your experience in this kind of work?" not "How much are your hourly fees?" The dollar amount of an hourly fee shrinks to insignificance compared to the value of your business.

14. The Other Thing

Although I titled this book *"11 Things You Absolutely Need to Know About Selling Your Business,"* I didn't mean that you need to know *only* 11 things in order to sell your business. There are a thousand small details that can make the transition to the next phase of your life more rewarding and less stressful.

There is one broad bit of advice I can render above any technical or industry expertise offered here. <u>PATIENCE</u>. According to a recent study, the average Main Street company is on the market for 22 months from listing to close.

I frequently get calls from owners who are "ready to sell." They have debated the move for years. Now that they finally have taken the step of calling an intermediary, they want to be rid of their company in 30 days or less. Many are very disappointed to discover that there is no giant international database of qualified, ready buyers with huge amounts of cash in hand.

Planning the sale of your business is a major undertaking. Like any business decision with a high potential for reward, it should be approached carefully and systematically. Quick sales are too often cheap sales.

The process of selling your business has many stages. It is easy to become frustrated by the time and energy that it takes. In a small company, there is a substantial danger that the distraction of dealing with prospects and their professional advisors can draw the owner away from running his or her business.

Be patient in the negotiations. Some intermediaries like to keep the pressure on to get things done. Offers and counteroffers are fired back and forth via email, with short deadlines for response. Don't get wrapped up in the "Do it now!" mentality. A good buyer will go through a process with you. A good intermediary will respect that this is a huge decision in your life.

Be patient with the prospects. Some will be shoppers; but only one has to be qualified. Remember that the buyer is likely to be risking his life savings. If his previous career was collecting a paycheck, generating his own income may be a terrifying thought that takes some getting used to. He may focus on the wrong things, or be dismissive of features in your business that you know are terrific. He will learn what is important about your business, because you will teach him that during the process.

Be patient with the requests for information from buyers and banks and landlords and vendors. They all must be satisfied to go through with the deal. They may know you, but they probably didn't know that you were planning on going away. They don't know the buyer, and may need some time to get comfortable with him.

Be patient with others around you who don't know, or don't realize, the level of distraction you will be dealing with. Your customers will still expect you to be responsive. Your employees will still have questions. Your family is not likely to understand what a huge change you are planning in your and their lives.

Most importantly, be patient with yourself. If you have never sold a company before, this will be a learning process for you as well. You won't know all the right questions. You will think that you understand something, only to find out that you misunderstood it. There will be days when you can't wait to get out the door, but no one else seems to be interested in making anything happen.

On other days, you'll decide that this is all a mistake, and that running the company for a few more years is a better idea. If you've written down all the things that you are going to do after the sale (see Chapter 4), take another look at it when your enthusiasm for moving on starts to waver.

It may not be easy, but selling your business is like cashing in your chips at the end of a successful night at the gaming tables. Looking back on it, you had some fun, you had some pain, and you are walking away with, more or less, the results you hoped for when you sat down.

Thank You

I hope this book is a help to you in preparing for the most important financial transaction of your life.

My special thanks go to my family, associates and brokerage team in San Antonio, to Barry Bankler, who introduced me into the brokerage business, to George Dawson, who missed his calling as an editor, to the folks at Robot Creative for making us look so good, and especially to the members and facilitators of The Alternative Board® (www.thealternativeboard.com), whose wisdom and experience can be found on every page of this book.

Over the years I've become more concerned with the preparedness of Baby Boomers to exit their businesses. Most owners who approach me about selling could have realized much, much higher prices if they had put a few more years into planning. I hope that this book helps you to realize that, even for the smallest business, selling your business is worth every ounce of preparation and effort that you can put into it.

Glossary of Terms

ABV: Accredited in Business Valuation. The credential offered by the American Institute of Certified Public Accountants

ASA: The American Society of Appraisers. Credentialing is in areas of specialty, including Business Valuation, Machinery and Technical Specialties, and Real Property.

AVA: Accredited Valuation Analyst. The credential of the National Association of Valuation analysts.

Biz Comps: A proprietary database of business sale prices and financial benchmarks. Requires paid membership.

Bizbuysell.com: A popular web site for listing businesses for sale.

BizQuest.com: A popular web site for listing businesses for sale.

Buyer's Sanity Check: Any formula or equation that calculates the ability of a business' cash flow to sustain debt service, provide income to the owner, and return "cash on cash" earnings for the capital invested.

C Corporation: The default for any corporate entity which hasn't elected a Subchapter S tax status.

CBI: Certified Business Intermediary. The professional designation of the International Business Brokers' Association

CBR: Confidential Business Review. A term for the document that describes the features and opportunities of a business for sale. Also called an offering memorandum, although that term has become more associated with investment capital.

CExP: Certified Exit Planner. The designation of the Business Enterprise Institute for professionals who complete approximately 120 hours of coursework in exit planning, especially regarding transfers to family and employees.

CMEA: Certified Machinery and Equipment Appraiser. The designation of the National Equipment and Business Builders Institute

Craig's List: A website offering low and no cost listings for things to buy and sell in most major cities

CVA: Certified Valuation Analyst. Another certification offered by the National Association of Valuation Analysts. (See AVA)

Dismal Ds: Ten bad things that happen to cause the sale of a business. They include Declining sales, Dissention among owners, Disinterest, Disaster, Distraction, Debt, Divorce, Disease, Disability, and Death.

EBIT: Earnings Before Interest and Taxes. A measure of cash flow.

EBITDA: Earnings Before Interest and Taxes, Depreciation or Amortization EBIT with added cash flow credited for non-cash deduction for capital expenditures or expenses that are written off over time.

Generation X: Generally, those born in the United States between 1966 and 1985. The term is variously attributed to the unknown characteristics of the generation, or to the fact that some calculate it to be the tenth generation born since US independence.

IRS: Internal Revenue Service. The branch of the Federal Government that collects taxes. (Like you didn't know!)

LLC: Limited Liability Company. An entity structure that combines some features of both partnership and corporations.

LDC: Local Development Corporation. A quasi-governmental entity tasked with helping small businesses start and obtain SBA funding.

M&A: Merger and Acquisition. The general term for the industry focused on the buying and selling of businesses. More frequently used in mid-market, large and publicly traded transactions.

Main Street: The general term for small businesses selling for under $2,000,000.

Mid-Market: Privately held companies with professional management and systems. Most often in excess of $10,000,000 in revenues, and selling for over $3,000,000.

PEG: Private Equity Group. A vehicle for investors to pool their funds and purchase companies

Pratt's Stats: A proprietary database of business sale prices and financial benchmarks. Requires paid membership.

ProfitCents: A proprietary database of financial statistics about businesses. Requires paid membership.

RMA: Risk Management Association (formerly Robert Morris Associates.) A proprietary database of financial statistics about businesses. Requires paid membership.

ROI: Return on Investment: The calculation of the rate of payback on a given sum invested for the purpose of making money.

S Corporation: An election to have a corporation's income passed through to the owner(s) for taxation purposes.

SBA: Small Business Administration. The Federal Government's department for small businesses, most commonly known for its guarantee of bank loans.

SBIC: Small Business Investment Corporation: An SBA governed entity that works under special rules to directly invest money in small businesses.

SDCF: Seller's Discretionary Cash Flow. A measure of profitability which includes operating profit, owner's benefits and non0cash items

SDE: Seller's Discretionary Earnings. Synonymous with SDCF.

USPAP: Uniform Standards of Appraisal Practice. The rule making body for most certified appraisers.

WIIFM: What's In It For Me? A mnemonic for business owners to remember the difference between features and benefits.

About the Author:

John F. Dini, CMBA, CExP, CBI, CMPE, CPBA

John F. Dini has over 30 years of experience as a serial entrepreneur, and is currently running his seventh business. He has owned and operated successful start-up and turnaround companies for over 30 years.

He is a Certified MBA, and holds additional credentials as an Exit Planner, Business Intermediary, Business Broker, Medical Practice Executive, and Professional Behavioral Analyst, as well as a Facilitator and Business Coach.

John founded The Alternative Board® in San Antonio, Texas in 1997 and oversaw its growth to the most successful chapter in the world. He writes on small business ownership for newspapers and magazines, and speaks frequently to business owner groups. His small business advice blog can be found at www.awakeat2oclock.com.

MPN Advisors LLC, a subsidiary of MPN Inc.
12015 Radium St. San Antonio, TX 78216
T: (210) 615-1800 F: (210) 615-1865
JDini@mpninc.com
www.mpninc.com

"11 Things You Absolutely Need to Know About Selling Your Business"

is also an interactive seminar available for your business organization or association. Please contact us for additional information.

Praise for the First Edition of

11 Things You Absolutely Need to Know About Selling Your Business

Reading the "11 Things" will be one of the best investments in time anyone thinking about selling their business can make. The booklet points out things that most business owners don't know -- but absolutely need to know-- about selling their business. –

Allen E. Fishman, Author, Syndicated Columnist, Founder & CEO
TAB Boards International

Whenever someone asks my advice about selling their business, I tell them two things: First, get as much education about the process as possible. And second, "Don't try this at home -- get professional help!" As to the first part, you can't do better than this handy jewel co-authored by my friend, John Dini. It's short -- to compensate for an entrepreneur's attention span. And it's comprehensive -- to deliver all the stuff you need to know. Thanks, John and Carlos, for making this process so easy. As to the second part, is there and part of "Don't try this at home!" that's unclear? –

Jim Blasingame, Award-winning host of the nationally syndicated
"Small Business Advocate" radio show,
Best-selling author and syndicated columnist.

I have purchased many of these books to share with my clients who have found it very useful. It sets out a road map you can use on how to deal with the various people you need on your team in order to make sure you have a successful deal.

Jacquelyn Gernaey, Author and Business Coach

Long Island, New York

Even after reading it, I don't know how the author provided such a comprehensive tutorial so concisely. This one will surprise you. It goes beyond the basics of valuing your business, seeking buyers, and negotiating, to include really sound advice on some of the less obvious strategies involved in a successful sale.

Douglas Roof, Hockessin, Delaware

This short book is packed with practical, useful advice. The insights come from 2 gentlemen who have not only been there and done that, but they've written the book and share what you must do to successfully sell your business. They've managed to condense a weighty subject into just the essentials you need to know.

Carl Ammaccapane, Detroit, Michigan

It isn't everyday that you sell your business and John Dini takes something that is complex and sometimes overwhelming and breaks it down into basic steps that provide a road map for the reader.

Blair Koch, Denver, Colorado

The authors have described the "must know" of selling a business in a very practical form. The 11 things are in the category of "I should have known it" but many times (if not always) escape the attention of the business owner.

Oswald Viva, Philadelphia, Pennsylvania

You can't go wrong in making such a minor investment for the type of knowledge that will have such a major impact on your results.

Tina Corner, Annapolis, Maryland

CPSIA information can be obtained at www.ICGtesting.com
Printed in the USA
LVOW101559180113

316319LV00022B/920/P